A STUDENT'S APPROACH TO WORLD RELIGIONS

Christianity

D0234070

A STUDENT'S APPROACH TO WORLD RELIGIONS

Christianity

Brian E. Close and Marion Smith

SERIES EDITOR : BRIAN E. CLOSE

Hodder & Stoughton

LONDON SYDNEY AUCKLAND

British Library Cataloguing in Publication Data
Close, Brian E.
 Christianity: Student's Approach to World Religions
 I. Title II. Smith, Marion
 200
 ISBN 0-340-54692-1

First published 1992

Typeset by Litho Link Ltd, Welshpool, Powys.
Printed in Great Britain for the educational publishing division of Hodder & Stoughton
Ltd, Mill Road, Dunton Green, Sevenoaks, Kent by Clays Ltd, St Ives plc.

ACKNOWLEDGEMENTS

My grateful thanks for information and
suggestions and criticism to the Bishop of
Huntingdon and Mrs Roe, to Mr David
Prince, Headmaster of Reed's School, and to
Mr K.M. Kratt, Proprietor of The Bookmark,
Cobham.

B.C.

The publishers would like to thank the following for permission to
reproduce material in this volume:

Burns & Oates Ltd for the extract from History of the Church,
Volume V: Reformation and Counter Reformation by H. Jedin;
SCM Press for the extract from Questioning Christian Origins by
J.K. Elliott.

The cover photograph has been supplied by the Bridgeman Art
Library.

PREFACE

This book is primarily intended to help students preparing for GCE A-Level Examinations in Christianity, although it will provide a valuable introduction for undergraduates reading the subject in great depth, and assistance to others wishing to increase their background knowledge.

The book is divided into a number of Topics which appear regularly in Examination Syllabuses. Within each Topic the subject matter is carefully arranged and technical terms explained.

It is not possible in a short book to deal adequately with all aspects of the Topics covered but our aim has been to provide a bridge between GCSE and the study of specialist books. We hope that the information given will enable students to make constructive use of the latter.

AUTHORSHIP

Chapters one to five of this book have been written by Brian Close, and chapters six to nine by Marion Smith.

CONTENTS

INTRODUCTION

The centre of Christianity is the person Jesus of Nazareth who was born in Palestine under the Roman Emperor Augustus (27BCE–14CE), appeared in public under his successor Tiberius (14–37 CE), and was executed by the governor ('procurator') of Judaea, Pontius Pilate (26–36 CE). For a man who so changed the course of history that people began to date the years of the world from his birth, we have little information concerning Jesus. There are the early Roman and Jewish sources (chapter one), but these report scarcely anything that is useful beyond the fact that he truly existed. For our knowledge of Jesus we are dependent upon the tradition of the Church as this is set forth in the books of the New Testament and particularly in the four Gospels. The historian who is interested in Jesus as an historical figure, as well as the Christian who is concerned about the historical basis of his faith, are both faced with a twofold task; to examine critically what is written and to determine the purpose of the individual writer in his own culture. In chapters one to three we shall investigate the proclamation of, and about, Jesus, and the narratives that go with it.

In our study of the Church in history it is impracticable to follow the chronological sequence of events over nearly 2000 years. The synopsis of such a history in the space available would be so condensed as to be misleading. Instead we shall examine significant turning-points which help us to understand both how and why the Church has developed in the way that it has done.

Obviously, none of these chapters represents the last word on the topic in question.

Abbreviations

BCE	Before Common Era (= B.C.)	Jer	Jeremiah
CE	Common Era (= A.D.)	Jn	John
cf.	contrast	Lev	Leviticus
chap	chapter	Lk	Luke
2 Chr	2 Chronicles	Mal	Malachi
1 Cor	1 Corinthians	Mic	Micah
cp.	compare	Mk	Mark
Dtr	Deuteronomy	Mt	Matthew
e.g.	for example	Num	Numbers
Ex	Exodus	OT	Old Testament
Ezek	Ezekiel	par.	parallels
Gal	Galatians	Ps	Psalms
Gen	Genesis	Rev	Revelation
i.e.	in other words	Rom	Romans
Isa	Isaiah	1 Sam	1 Samuel
		Zech	Zechariah

CHAPTER ONE

JESUS: SOURCES AND PROCLAMATION

What do we know about Jesus? How do we evaluate sources of information about him? Can we distinguish historical information from the proclamation of the religious significance of Jesus made by his followers? There are basic questions we need to ask as we examine the New Testament.

The words of Jesus (the *logia*), and the proclamation (*kerygma*) of Jesus as Lord and Christ, were at first handed on and repeated orally. In the second half of the 1st and during the early decades of the 2nd century this oral tradition was written down in the form of letter-writing, gospel, theological narrative, homiletic and apocalyptic literature. Those writings believed to have been penned by an apostle, or to have the authority of an apostle behind them, were collected for use by the whole Church. It took a long time for some of the books to achieve universal recognition. For example, the Letter to the Hebrews was under suspicion in the West until the 4th century because of doubts (now accepted as correct) as to whether St. Paul wrote it. In his Easter Letter for the year 367, Bishop Athanasius of Alexandria is the first to cite the 27 books of the present New Testament as alone canonical. His list was officially recognised at the Council of Carthage in 397.

The Pauline Letters

The oldest extant documents of the New Testament are the Letters of Paul which were written in the CE 50's. In the main, these letters are pastoral letters written to individual churches in Paul's care, i.e. they are addressed to communities of Christians and their purpose is to give clear guidance relevant to the needs of each particular community. For example, in his First Letter to the Corinthian Church, Paul deals with such diverse matters as, Christians dividing the church into rival parties, a member of the church living in immorality, women wearing veils in church, and what Paul regards as false teaching about the resurrection of the dead.

The influence of Paul is visible in *1 Clement*, written to Corinth towards the end of the first century, which cites his career and martyrdom to urge unity in the congregation. Ignatius of Antioch (beginning of the second century) and Polycarp (died c156) both honoured and used Paul's letters. However, the apostle was also suspect in many quarters because of the use of his thought by Gnostic Christians (see chapter 5).

Paul was not one of the original eye-witnesses of Jesus, though he had access to a good many people who had known him personally. He rarely alludes to Jesus' teaching, and does not show any particular concern for Jesus' biography. Apart from the Last Supper, crucifixion, and various resurrection appearances (the tradition which he himself has received and is handing on: *1 Cor* 11:23ff; 15:3ff; *Phil* 2:6-11), Paul supplies little information about Jesus' life. His interest lay rather in the theological significance of the death, resurrection, exaltation and coming of Jesus for the believer now: 'For him, "the life of Jesus" was primarily the life that followed the crucifixion and resurrection', a new mode of life that 'carried the promise of life for all who were his' (Dr A.M.Hunter).

The Gospels

The principal sources for the life of Jesus are the four Gospels (Old English, *godspel*, 'good news'): Matthew, Mark, Luke and John. Although there may be historical tradition underlying these, it must be remembered that their purpose is to convey the 'good news' of Jesus, rather than transmit historical information as such. Each evangelist has his own particular way of seeing Jesus' ministry. In order to distinguish the separate Gospels they are described as 'the Gospel *according to* Matthew', 'the Gospel *according to* Mark', and so on. Because they readily admit a parallel view of their sources, Matthew, Mark and Luke are termed the 'synoptic' Gospels.

The majority of opinion among scholars is that Mark's is the earliest Gospel, written between 65-75 CE when many who remembered the events must still have been alive; that both Matthew and Luke used Mark as a primary source (all but 31 verses of Mark are found in either Matthew or Luke, or both), as well as drawing upon a collection of Jesus' sayings (often called 'Q': German, *Quelle*, 'source') unknown to Mark; that John's Gospel came last (written about 95-100 CE) but drew upon a much greater mass of evidence than the synoptics (see *John* 20:30; 21:25). The principal alternative to this view is probably the Griesbach Hypothesis (for J.J. Griesbach, 1745–1812), which dates Matthew first, sees it as a source for Luke, and regards both Matthew and Luke as sources for Mark. Other theories are more complex, suggesting successive revisions of one or more of the Gospels to account for the similarities. The important point is that there is dispute about which Gospel came first, and there are no easy answers.

Although the Gospels were probably composed at a relatively late date they draw their material from a much older oral tradition, recited and repeated by the earliest disciples. Indeed, it is precisely because they are held to contain the apostolic proclamation (*kerygma*) that the Gospels are valued so highly by the Church.

The Early Proclamation

In his book *The Apostolic Preaching and its Developments*, Professor C.H.Dodd attempted to reconstruct an outline of the apostolic proclamation from the 'primitive' material which he believed is preserved in the speeches of Peter and Paul in *Acts* (2:14-39; 3:13-26; 4:10-12; 5:30-32; 10:36-43; 13:17-41) and in those passages in the Pauline Letters where Paul seems to be using the traditional formulas (esp. *1 Cor* 15:1-7; *Rom* 1:1-4; 8:34, 10:8-9). The message is as follows:

> The promises made in the Old Testament are fulfilled.
> The Messiah son of David has come.
> He is Jesus of Nazareth, who
> > Went about doing good and executing mighty works
> > > by the power of God,
> > Was crucified according to the purpose of God,
> > Was raised by God from the dead,
> > Is exalted by God and given the name Lord,
> > Will come again for the judgement and restoration
> > > of all things,
> Therefore all you who hear the message repent and be baptised.

The earliest disciples were therefore united in their common faith that 'Jesus is Messiah' and the fact upon which this faith relied was the death of Jesus and belief in his resurrection.

Recent scholarship, however, has questioned the validity of the historical approach of Luke-Acts. The speeches in *Acts* are 'Lucan' creations or the author has so completely rewritten his sources that it is impossible to know what is primitive material in them. Much will depend upon whether the traditional view of the authorship of Luke-Acts, that it was by a companion of St. Paul (and therefore to be dated in the first century), is correct. Since the work is anonymous, internal indications must be sought. Parts of *Acts* 16-28 are written in the first person plural, suggesting that the author was a participant in the journeys of Paul and was not simply using the conventional 'we': 16:10-17, 20:5-15; 21:1-18, 27:1-28:16, and 11:28 in Codex Bezae (a 5th century manuscript). It is interesting that other ancient historical writings made use of the first person plural in narrations of journeys to indicate participation see, e.g. Lucian, *History* 47. Some scholars have questioned this conclusion, noting that were the author a companion of Paul, he would probably have shown awareness of Paul's letters and major teachings and ascribed the title of apostle to Paul, who always so referred to himself. Also, the author's picture of the early Church cannot easily be reconciled with that gleaned from the Pauline letters: 'The Council of Acts 15 remains enigmatic; if Peter had already had the full experience of the Cornelius episode, it remains very hard indeed to understand the Antioch incident of Galatians 2:11-14,' (Eric Franklin, *Christ the Lord*, p176). E. Haenchen (*The Book of Acts as Source Material for the History of Early Christianity*) believes that the problem here is caused, not by lack of sources or an inadequate appreciation of the historical situation, but by the subordination by Luke of his history to his theology. For Franklin, this is the fundamental factor and one which does not concern Luke's competence, but his purpose:

> "The Lucan picture of unity, of harmony, of unimpeded progress, and of the Jewishness of what emerged, was caused, not by practical historical problems which faced the new community, but by his theological belief that this community was the eschatological people of God, the heirs of God's promises and the fulfilment of Old Testament expectations. This controlled his descriptions in Acts in exactly the same manner that it controlled his Gospel. There, the life of Jesus, his 'historical' progress to Jerusalem, his resurrection appearances, and his ascension, are all the outcome of theological presuppositions which determine also the nature of the infancy narratives. In his second volume, too, the history is written 'from faith to faith' to express the conviction that what has emerged is really what it ought to be, that it is determined by the purposes of God. Luke knows what the community is; his work describes its emergence as his vision of this dictates it." (Franklin, above cit., pp 176, 177).

A Single Narrative

While the events surrounding the Passion (Latin, *passio*, 'suffering')
provided the nucleus of the earliest Gospel, they were not the whole
of it. At *Acts* 2:22 (also 10:38), St. Peter speaks of: "Jesus of Nazareth,
a man singled out by God and made known to you through miracles,
portents and signs, which God worked among you through him, as
you well know . . ." It is likely that the oral tradition soon prefixed to
the Passion story other events of Jesus' ministry that were important
for the Church's faith in him. And the teaching of Jesus had an
immensely practical relevance to the life of the Church. Once new
members has been added to the fold, a new life-style was demanded
of them; Christian instructors would surely need Jesus' teaching as
the authority for the discipline they were seeking to impose. The
need for this teaching would be most acute in areas where large
numbers of converts began to be drawn from non-Jewish circles.

It is widely accepted that it was St. Mark who first joined the
traditions together editorially, imposing a geographical and
chronological framework on Jesus' ministry. He thereby created the
impression of a connected chain of events, although, in fact, many of
the traditions may well have reached him without any indication of
date, place, or historical circumstances. Mark's work was never
intended to be an historical narrative which merely reproduced the
story of Jesus. He was writing a Gospel, a call to faith in Jesus Christ
the son of God (see 1:1). He wrote to proclaim who Jesus is for all
generations of men to come, i.e. his purpose was theological.

What Mark offers is a certain view of Jesus' ministry based on the
historical tradition. The same is true of each of the Gospel writers.
All are united in proclaiming Jesus as Messiah but their emphases
and interests are not the same. It could hardly be otherwise when the
communities out of which and for which the Gospels were written
were so richly diverse.

Summary

The traditions concerning Jesus were preserved orally in the
worshipping life of the Christian community. Inevitably, selections
were made to answer the Church's needs in preaching and teaching,
and history, as we understand the term, was less important to them
than the proclamation of Jesus as risen Lord and Christ. Mark and
the other evangelists joined the traditions together editorially but

interpreted the material to meet the specific needs of their own churches. To question the historical accuracy of gospel material is not to challenge its value; to treat it only as historical information is to misunderstand its purpose.

The Non-Christian Evidence for Jesus

Few secular documents say anything about him. The principal authorities are Josephus, Tacitus, Suetonius and the Talmud.

1. Josephus

Josephus was born ben Matthias in 37 or 38 CE of a Jewish priestly family in Jerusalem, and was historian of the Jews at the courts of Vespasian, Titus and Domitian. Josephus had commanded the Galilean forces during the initial stages of the Jewish revolt (66-70 CE) but gave himself up to the Romans following the siege of Jotapata (67 CE). He was given his freedom when Vespasian was proclaimed emperor by his troops in 69 CE.

In his work, *Antiquitates Judaicea* ('The Antiquities of the Jews'), completed in twenty books in 93 CE, Josephus traces the history of the Jews from the creation of the world to the outbreak of the Jewish-Roman war. In Book XX, he writes about a High Priest Ananus who "assembled the Sanhedrin and brought before them James, the brother of Jesus, who was called Christ . . ." (XX.9.200). Note the derogatory "who was called" (i.e. the 'so-called' Christ). Josephus the Jew knows well enough that 'Christ' (Latin, *christus*) is synonymous with 'Messiah' (Hebrew, *mashiah*, 'The Anointed One') and he will not accept the notion of Jesus' messiahship. This is important for an earlier passage in the 'Antiquities' (known as 'The Testimony of Flavius', i.e. Flavius Josephus) where the messiahship of Jesus is affirmed:

> "Now there was about this time Jesus, a wise man, if it be lawful to call him a man, for he was a doer of wonderful works, a teacher of such men as receive the truth with pleasure. He drew over to him both many of the Jews, and many of the Gentiles, He was the Christ. And when Pilate, at the suggestion of the principal men amongst us, had condemned him to the cross, those that loved him at the first did not forsake him; for he appeared to them alive again at the third day; as the divine prophets had foretold these and ten thousand other wonderful

things concerning him. And the tribe of Christians, so named from him, are not extinct at this day," (XVIII. 3.63-64).

Josephus could not have written the statements in both books. What we do know is that here was a historian of the Jews who had by no means abandoned his Judaism even though he was loathed by the Jews as a traitor. Consequently, scholars are generally of the opinion that this 'Testimony of Flavius' is not authentic but represents the work of a later Christian copyist who modified what Josephus had written. If this is correct, then Christian hands worked over the passage at a relatively early date because in its present form 'The Testimony of Flavius' is known by Eusebius, Bishop of Caesarea c260-c340.

2. Tacitus

Tacitus (full Latin name, Gaius Cornelius Tacitus; c56-120 CE), was a Roman historian and high official in the imperial government. His major works are the *Historiae* ('Histories'), the history of the empire from the accession of Galba in 68 CE to the assassination of Domitian in 96, and the later *Annales* ('Annals'), a history of the Julian line from Tiberius to Nero (14 to 68 CE).

In the *Annales* (XV.44; written about 110 CE), Tacitus mentions the persecution of the Christians by the emperor Nero who, he says, made them scapegoats for the fire of Rome (64 CE): "Nero fastened the guilt and inflicted the most exquisite tortures on a class hated for their abominations, called Christians by the populace. Christus, from whom the name had its origin, suffered the extreme penalty during the reign of Tiberius at the hands of one of our procurators, Pontius Pilate, and a pernicious superstition, thus checked for the moment, again broke out not only in Judea, the first source of the evil, but also in Rome, where all things hideous and shameful from every part of the world meet and become popular . . ."

3. Suetonius

Suetonius (full Latin name, Gaius Suetonius Tranquillus; born in Rome c69 CE), was an historian and biographer. Chief among his writing is *De vita Caesarum* ('The Lives of the Caesars') from Julius Caesar to Domitian. The following passage from his 'Life of Claudius' (*Vita Claudii* 25.4; written after 100 CE) is generally held to refer to the riots of 49 CE among the Jews of Rome, brought on by the intrusion of Christianity into the synagogues:

"Since the Jews constantly made disturbances at the instigation of Chrestus, he (Claudius) expelled them from Rome."

As many of the early Christians were Jews, it was easy for the authorities to confuse the two groups and view the disturbances as a Jewish quarrel. Suetonius says *Chrestus* instead of *Christus*, but pronunciation of the two names in Latin is very close. Claudius' edict of expulsion is referred to in Acts 18:2.

4. Talmud

According to the *Talmud* (a compendium of Jewish law, lore and commentary), Jesus, (Hebrew, *Yeshu*) was begotten of an adulteress (Miriam, or Mary) with a Roman soldier (variously called Pandera, Pantera or Panthera). He had five disciples (Mattai, Nakkai, Netzer, Buni and Todah), stirred up the people, worked healings and sorcery, ridiculed the wise, and was hanged (crucified) on the eve of Passover. The appellation 'Yeshu the Nazarene' leaves us in no doubt that this is the Jesus of the Gospels. The story appears to have been in circulation about 150 CE.

Conclusion

The non-Christian evidence for Jesus is meagre and adds nothing to our knowledge of what he said or did. Even so, these independent accounts are not unimportant. What they prove is that in the first century CE even the opponents of Christianity never doubted his existence as a human being. This is sufficient ground for rejecting outright the notion of Jesus having been a purely mythical or invented figure.

CHAPTER TWO

JESUS: TEACHING AND MINISTRY

From the beginning, Christians were reflecting upon the meaning of what Jesus had been and what he had said and done, and proclaiming that belief in witness and worship. The Gospel writers are themselves believers looking back and presenting the already-developed understanding of the Christian Church. It follows that if we are to understand the Gospel accounts of Jesus we have to consider the faith of the early Church regarding him. We have to consider, too, the contribution of the individual Gospel writer in his treatment and presentation of the traditions. Each of the Gospels is an independent whole, for each writer selects and arranges the material to suit his own purpose and readership. The result is that each Gospel has its own special contribution to make to the picture of Jesus with which the New Testament confronts us.

The Witness of John the Baptist

Each of the Gospels precedes Jesus' public ministry with an account of John the Baptist, thereby underlining John's importance in the proclamation of Christian faith.

Mark emphasises John's 'Elijah role' (*Mk* 1:6 reminiscent of *2 Kings* 1:8) as the forerunner of the mighty one (*Mk* 1:7; i.e. the eschatological deliverer) in accordance with Old Testament prophecy. According to Malachi, the messenger is sent to prepare the way before the Lord comes with judgement (*Mal* 3.2f.). John accordingly preaches a baptism of repentance with a view to the forgiveness of sins (*Mk* 1:4). It may be that John's baptism has as its background Jewish proselyte-baptism. Gentile converts were baptised to show that they had thrown off the evils of their past lives. However, John's baptism is of a more decisive character: he demands not only a complete turning away from sin but changed lives. Note how Mark stresses 'the vast superiority' (Cranfield) of the one who comes: John is not worthy to stoop down and untie the thong of his sandals, a task so degrading that no Jew ought to perform it for another (cf. Rabbi Joshua ben Levi, "All services which a slave does for his master a pupil should do for his teacher, with the exception of undoing his shoes"). The contrast between the two is also to be seen in their actions: John baptises with water, the coming one will baptise with the Holy Spirit. One of the signs of the last age was to be the outpouring of the Spirit on all flesh (*Joel* 2:28).

Matthew and Luke are both more interested in what John said than in what he stands for.

In *Matthew* 3:2 the words, "Repent, for the kingdom of heaven is at hand", are sibstituted for Mark's, 'preaching a baptism of repentance for the forgiveness of sins' (*Mk* 1.4). The keynote is judgement: the one who will follow him, John says, will hold in his hand a winnowing fork, 'and he will clear his threshing floor and gather his wheat into the granary, but the chaff he will burn with unquenchable fire' (*Mt*: 3.12). John rebukes those who pride themselves on being descended from Abraham, and says that 'God is able from these stones to raise up children to Abraham' (*Mt* 3:9). In Aramaic the words 'children' and 'stones' are almost identical.

Luke extends the Marcan quotation from *Isaiah* 40 to enable a universal reference to be included, 'and all flesh shall see the salvation of God' (*Isa* 40:5). Luke alone gives details of the ethical teaching of John in which he explains what is meant by 'fruits that befit repentance' in practical terms (3.8, 10-14). He notes the reaction of the crowd who wonder if John himself were the Christ and uses it to prepare his readers for John's next statement about the mightier one.

A different picture of John is given in the fourth Gospel. He is not himself the Christ or Elijah or the prophet, but only preparing the way for one greater, merely a 'voice' (*Jn* 1.23). Notice the triple denial in 1:20, 21, showing the need that still existed of guarding against an exaggeration of John's position. Even towards the end of the first century, when the Gospel was written, there were some who venerated John and considered him above Jesus himself. The fourth Gospel represents Jesus and John as working side by side for a time, until Jesus begins to make more disciples than John and the latter voluntarily withdraws, saying, "He must increase, but I must decrease." (*Jn* 3:30)

The Baptism of Jesus

Mark's account of the baptism is related entirely as Jesus's own experience. The narrative is brief; Mark is content to set down the tradition and he allows it to speak for himself. The vital elements in the story are the opening of the heavens, the descent of the Spirit, and the words of the voice: "Thou art my beloved Son: with thee I am well pleased" (*Mk* 1:11). 'The heavens opened' is symbolic language for the receiving of a vision or revelation from God (cp. *Ezekiel* 1.1). The phrase 'like a dove' is metaphorical, not suggesting that an actual dove appeared. A first-century rabbinic interpretation compared the Spirit of God 'moving over the face of the waters' (*Genesis* 1:2) to a dove 'which broods over her young but does not trouble them'. If Mark was aware of this interpretation, then the meaning of it may well be that as at the creation of the world the Spirit of God was at work, bringing order out of chaos, so now, Jesus is the centre of a new creative activity by the Spirit. The words of the voice are addressed to Jesus alone; their purpose is, at least in part, to give the reader the secret of Jesus' identify, but the use of *Psalm* 2:7 and *Isaiah* 42:1 may well be Mark's way of enlisting the support of the Old Testament to designate this start of Jesus' ministry as a new work of creation. The notion of redemption as a new creation brought about in Christ through the work of the Spirit had been expressed by Paul in *Romans* 8.

Mark's Gospel gives no indication that the Baptist paid Jesus special attention, but Matthew has John protest: "I need to be baptised by you, and do you come to me?" Jesus reassures him: "Let it be so now; for thus it is fitting for us to fulfil all righteousness," (*Mt* 3.14-15). It may be that Matthew has added the conversation in order to answer certain questions concerning the baptism which Mark's account raised: 'Why should Jesus be baptised if John's baptism was for the remission of sins?' 'Could Jesus be inferior to John given that he *submits* himself to John's baptism?' Canon Fenton notes: "Part of Matthew's purpose in writing his Gospel was to overcome difficulties which had been raised by the work of his predecessor, and the addition of these verses seems to be an explanation of this kind" (J.C. Fenton, *Saint Matthew*, p59).

Luke's account is similar to Mark's, but with the characteristic addition that Jesus 'was praying' (*Lk* 3.21). It seems that whenever Luke wants his readers to realise that an event is particularly important in Jesus's life, he informs us that Jesus was praying, thereby underlining the readiness of Jesus to align himself with the will of God (see 6:12, 9:18, 9:28, 11:1, 22:41).

The fourth Gospel does not record that Jesus was baptised.

The Ministry of Jesus

A. Jesus as preacher and teacher

In Mark, a summary statement of his preaching at the beginning of the proclamation is evidently intended to characterise Jesus' ministry as a whole (1:15): "The time is fulfilled, and the kingdom of God is at hand; repent, and believe in the gospel." According to Matthew and Luke, when Jesus extended his mission by sending out his disciples in turn, it was the same message which he gave them (*Mt* 10:7; *Lk* 10:9). Moreover, the largest single group of parables are those which begin, 'The kingdom of God/heaven is like . . .'

Clearly, the Jewish eschatological concept 'Kingdom of God' is central to the Synoptic account of Jesus' preaching. An accurate understanding of the significance of the term for Jesus' hearers requires that we ask about its meaning in the Jewish background. In his commentary on *St. Mark* (p63f), Professor Cranfield points out that in the Old Testament the kingship of God is perceived in two main ways:

1   God is believed to be even now the King of Israel (*1 Sam* 12:12; *Isa* 41:21, 43:15) and of all nations (*Jer* 10:7; *Mal* 1:14). But the statement of God's kingly rule was sharply questioned by Israel's disobedience and disloyalty. So we arrive at

2   a second group of passages, in which God's kingly rule is referred to in terms of expectation and hope, as something yet to be realised (eg. *Zech* 14:9, 'And the Lord will become king over all the earth; on that day the Lord will be one and his name one.').

Cranfield also notes three features in the Rabbinic background that are important for our present understanding:-

(i)   The expression 'kingdom of heaven'. *Heaven* is a Jewish circumlocution for God; so in the Gospels Matthew's 'kingdom of heaven' is the more Jewish form, and therefore likely to be what Jesus used. *Kingdom* reflects the tendency in late Judaism to avoid using verbal expressions of God and to use abstract nouns instead. So the phrase 'Kingdom of God' in the Gospels means not something spatial (i.e. the area or the people over which God reigns), but rather describes God's function (his rule, his acting as king).

(ii)   The references to the kingdom's 'being revealed', which "express vividly the meaning of the eschatological thought of the kingship of God. At present God's rule is in a real sense hidden; but it is to become manifest and unambiguous".

(iii)   The references to 'receiving' (and 'throwing off') 'the kingdom' (or 'the yoke of the kingdom') 'of heaven'. "It is because God's rule is at present hidden that men are in a position to decide whether they will receive or reject it; and the fact that the day is coming when it will be made manifest makes that decision a matter of urgency".

The apparent paradox between the present ('already now') and the future ('not yet') aspects of the kingdom is clearly reflected in the Gospels:-

(a)   The Kingdom of God has come near; it has come upon those to whom Jesus is speaking (*Mk* 12:28 = *Lk* 11:20); it is in their midst (*Lk* 17:21). Cranfield observes, 'That which for the Old Testament was in the future, the object of hope, is now present.'

(b)   Yet, in other places, the kingdom is conceived as something in the future. Jesus' followers are to pray, 'Thy kingdom come' (*Mt* 6:10); the apostles are told that Jesus 'will not drink of the fruit of the vine until the kingdom of God comes' (*Lk* 22:18).

Two other important points which emerge from the Gospel traditions of the kingdom are:-

(c)   It is intimately bound up with Jesus' own person. When charged with using the power of Beelzebul to drive out demons, an alternative explanation of Jesus' power is given: "If it is by the Spirit of God that I cast out demons, then the kingdom of God has come upon you" (*Mt* 12:28 = *Lk* 11:20). Men who ask for a 'sign' are told: "The kingdom of God is not coming with signs to be observed; nor will they say, 'Lo, here it is!' or 'There!' for behold, the kingdom of God is in the midst of you" (*Lk* 17.20-21). In Jesus, the Kingdom of God is in operation now. As Cranfield observes, 'it is because he is in their midst that it is in their midst.'

(d)   The kingdom invites a personal response. It is first of all God's gift to humankind (*Lk* 12:32; *Mt* 21:43) but then it is up to men and women themselves to accept it or reject it and to take full responsibility for their own decisions. Cranfield notes 'the variety of terms by which men's relation to the kingdom is indicated. Of men it is said that they receive it (*Mk* 10:15 = *Lk* 18.17), wait for it (*Mk* 15:43 = *Lk* 23:51), inherit it (*Mt* 25:34), enter it (*Mt* 5:20, 7:21, 18:3 par., 19:23f. par., 23:13, *Mk* 9:47, *Mt* 21:31). It is also said that the kingdom belongs to certain people (*Mt* 5:3, 10; *Mk* 10:14). Men are summoned to seek it (*Lk* 12:31 = *Mk* 6:33), to strive to enter it (*Lk* 13:24: cf. *Mt* 7:14 which speaks of the gate and the way to life, a synonym for the kingdom); the rich young ruler is told to sell all and give to the poor in order to enter it (*Mk* 10:17f.). No sacrifice is too costly in order to win it (*Mt* 13:44-46; *Mk* 9:47).'

The parables are a major source for discovering the teaching of Jesus about the kingdom. Naturally, their interpretation is dependent on the view of the kingdom held by the individual writer. Albert Schweitzer, for instance, expounded them on the basis of 'thoroughgoing eschatology'. He held that Jesus shared with his contemporaries the expectation of a speedy end of the world, and in this was to be found the clue to the meaning of the parables of the kingdom. They referred to the imminent crisis prophesied by Jesus, e.g. it was in the suddenness of the rising of the leaven, not in its slow working, that the meaning of the parable of the leaven was to be found (*Mt* 13:33). By contrast, C.H. Dodd offered an interpretation which he described as 'realised eschatology'. He argued that the kingdom is realised in Jesus' word and deed, and saw this as the essential factor, even though he also accepted an eschatological element (in a future sense). Dodd therefore emphasised in the parables that which is realised in Jesus' activity, e.g. the mustard seed planted long ago had now become a tree (*Mk* 4.30-32). The German biblical scholar Joachim Jeremias has modified Dodd's approach. He speaks of an eschatology 'in process of realising itself'; for God's Kingdom is very close. According to Jeremias, the parables presented their hearers with a challenge, e.g. the parable of the unrighteous steward is a warning from Jesus to his contemporaries to take resolute and immediate action in the face of impending disaster (*Lk* 16.1-12). For Norman Perrin, the stress in Jesus's proclamation is that 'the experience of the present is an anticipation of the future'. In the parables of the sower, the mustard seed, and the leaven (*Mt* 13 par.) he sees, as do many other scholars, the contrast between the humble beginning and the expected powerful results. The parables confirm Jesus' trust in 'God's future': God will legitimise Jesus' proclamation and ministry, and the parables are intended to convey this trust to the listeners.

Mark has the following parables: the sower (4:1-9), the seed growing (4:26-29), the mustard seed (4:30-32) and the vineyard (12:1-11).

Matthew has all these (except for the seed growing) and also: the tares (13:24-30), the leaven (13:33), the hidden treasure (13:44), the pearl-merchant (13:45-46), the dragnet (13:47-50), the unforgiving servant (18:21-35), the labourers in the vineyard (20:1-16), the two sons (21:28-31), the marriage feast (22:1-10), the man without a wedding garment (22:11-14), the ten maidens (25:1-13), the talents (25:14-30) and the sheep and the goats (25:31-46).

Luke has the Marcan parables (except the seed growing) and also: the two debtors (7:41-42), the good Samaritan (10:30-37), the friend at midnight (11:5-8), the foolish rich man (12:15-21), the fig tree (13:6-9), the leaven (13:20-21), the great supper (14:15-24), the tower-builder (14:28-30), the king going to war (14:31-32), the lost sheep (15:3-7), the lost coin (15:8-10), the prodigal son (15:11-32), the unrighteous steward (16:1-12), the rich man and Lazarus (16:19-31), the slave and his master (17:7-10), the unjust judge (18:1-8), the Pharisee and the tax-collector (18:10-14) and the pounds (19:11-27).

The Gospel of John is apparently lacking in parables of the kind found in the other Gospels, but C.H. Dodd and A.M. Hunter have drawn attention to a number of 'embedded parables': *Jn* 3:8, 29; 4:35–38; 5:19f; 8:35; 10:1-5; 11:9f; 12:24, 35f; 16:21. Nor should we overlook the figurative descriptions which Jesus uses of himself in this Gospel, e.g. 'the good shepherd', 'the true vine', 'the door', 'the light of the world', and 'the way, and the truth, and the life'.

B. Jesus as healer

Jesus was active in healing. Concerning the 'mighty acts' of Jesus, his 'miracles', Herbert Braun has pointed out that in the ancient world there was nothing unusual about narratives telling of the working of miracles. However, the unique thing about the 'mighty acts' of Jesus was that they were set in connection with and interpreted as a sign of the coming Kingdom of God, e.g. at the start of the Galilean ministry Mark sets call stories and healings alongside each other (*Mk* 1:16–2:14); Mark also places miracles for particular purposes after Jesus' teachings (cp. *Mk* 7:24-37; 8:22-26; 9:14-29).

Scholars have further pointed out that the miracles have a typological precedent in the Old Testament, e.g. the manna given to Israel in the desert is a 'type' of Jesus' miracle of feeding. In other cases the miracles attributed to Jesus are said to correspond to the eschatological expectations of late Judaism concerning the messianic age (e.g. *Isa* 35:5-6, 'Then the eyes of the blind shall be opened, and the ears of the deaf unstopped; then shall the lame man leap like a hart, and the tongue of the dumb sing for joy').

Braun himself will not 'in rationalistic bluntness' contest all that is reported concerning the miracles of Jesus, and especially not his miracles of healing. But neither is he prepared to see actual events in the nature miracles, 'in any case not in the manner in which these miracles are described in the text'. That Jesus healed the sick, which according to the understanding of first-century ideas was described as the driving out of demons, he considers 'highly probable'.

J.K. Elliott considers that, 'From the historical point of view it is very unlikely that any of the miracles are historic. These stories were inevitable additions to the accounts of Jesus' ministry just as similar miracles were attributed to Peter, Paul and other early Christians in Acts as they were working in imitation of Jesus. The thinking behind these stories seems to have been that if Jesus was who the Christians believed he was, then he must by definition have been able to perform miracles. Attempts to rationalise or demythologise the miracles are to be untrue to their original purpose of showing Jesus as a divinely inspired Messianic figure and thereby evoking faith in others. The miraculous element is native to these stories and is inherent in them' (*Questioning Christian Origins*, p47).

During the time when the miracle stories were being transmitted orally, they may have developed and been enlarged upon. What was originally a parable may have been transformed into an event. This seems to be what has happened with the fig tree: in Luke it is a parable (13:6-9); Mark and Matthew describe it as the miracle of the withering fig tree (*Mk* 11:12-14, 20-21; *Mt* 21:20-21). Professor Aulén comments, 'It would be more than simple boldness to think that anyone can determine the facts behind all of the different miracle stories.'

The miracles recorded in the Gospels are mainly acts of healing or exorcisms. The following are found in Mark: a man with 'an unclean spirit' in the synagogue at Capernaum (*Mk* 1:23-26), Peter's mother-in-law, of fever (1:30-31), a leper (1:40-45), a paralysed man in a house (2:1-12), a man with a withered hand in a synagogue (3:1-6), a demoniac east of the Sea of Galilee (5:1-20), a woman with a haemorrhage (5:25-34), Jairus' daughter (5:21-24, 35-43), a Phoenician woman's daughter (7.24-30), a deaf stammerer (7:32-37), a blind man at Bethsaida (8:22-26), an epileptic near Caesarea Philippi (9:14-29), blind Bartimaeus at Jericho (10:46-52), with frequent mention of sick and possessed people in various places.

Matthew has most of these and also the healing of a centurion's servant (*Mt* 8:5-13), two blind men, which may be an extension of the Bartimaeus story (9:27-31), and he mentions in passing a dumb man possessed by a demon and a blind and dumb man. He also says that Jesus healed the blind and the lame in the Temple courts at Jerusalem – a parenthesis in the middle of a Marcan narrative (21:14).

Luke includes many of Mark's narratives and also the healing of a centurion's servant (*Lk* 7:2-10), the son of a widow at Nain (7:11-17), an infirm woman in a synagogue (13:10-17), a man with dropsy in a Pharisee's house (14:1-6) and ten lepers, one of whom was a Samaritan (17:12-19).

In addition, there are three 'nature miracles' (a modern classification): the quelling of the storm on the lake (*Mk* 4:35-41), the walking on the water (*Mk* 6:45-52) and the feeding of the people (*Mk* 6:30-44 and 8:1-10; generally considered as variant accounts of the same incident).

John avoids the Greek words used in the Synoptics which are translated 'works' and 'wonders'. There are none of the Synoptic acts of healing and no accounts of exorcism. Instead there are narrated seven 'signs': the turning of water into wine at Cana (2:1-11), the healing of a nobleman's son (4:46-54), the healing of the lame man at Jerusalem (5:1f), the feeding of the people (6:1-11), the walking on the water (6:16-21), the healing of a man born blind (9:1f), the raising of Lazarus (11:1f). Through the signs Jesus manifests his glory and his disciples perceive it, i.e. they are clear indications that Jesus is the Son of God.

C. Jesus as critic

Jesus' work led him into controversy. Primarily at issue was his behaviour, his way of acting. Scholars have noted four categories of acts which were attacked:-

(i)   Acts which involved violation of the law; not only of the contemporary interpretation of the law, but also of 'the law of Moses'. In the Gospels, those who most correctly observe the purity laws but at the same time neglect the fundamental principles of charity, sincerity, and humility (e.g. prayer, fasting, almsgiving,

sacrifice) are often severely criticised. The same sort of
condemnation is also found in contemporary Judaism, not least in
the Essenes (an ascetic sect living on the shore of the Dead Sea). But
while the Essenes attempted to sharpen the purity laws, Jesus'
concern was radically different: "there is nothing outside a man
which by going into him can defile him; but the things which come
out of a man are what defile him" (Mk 7:15; 'Of its genuineness there
can be no doubt', says Cranfield). Such a saying stood in opposition
to large tracts of the Torah which presuppose that as well as moral
cleanliness there is also a purely ritual cleanliness and that its
maintenance is of the utmost importance to God. The religious
establishment found this indifferent attitude of Jesus to the laws of
purification deeply disturbing. It was also, in different ways,
softened in the tradition which was later developed by the Gospel
text (Mk 7.18-23).

Scholars have detected the same relation between an original
radicalism in Jesus and a subsequent softening in the tradition in the
controversy over the proper observance of the Sabbath. They point
out that when Jesus healed the sick in defiance of the rabbinic
principle that only where life was at stake might the Sabbath law be
set aside, he did so regardless of whether his action could be
defended by any casuistic course of reasoning, e.g. 'to omit to do the
good which one could do to someone in need is to do evil'. Jesus'
radicalism was clearly expressed in the words: "The Sabbath was
made for man, not man for the Sabbath" (Mk 2:27). Aulén notes:
'With this he declared, in cutting opposition to Jewish thought, that
the Sabbath with its many rules was not a religious end in itself and
was not intended to serve God'. It is characteristic that, in different
ways, the radicalism of Jesus was softened and modified in the
subsequent tradition. For example, Jesus' behaviour was defended
by a reference to the action of King David who, when pressed by
hunger and hardship, had frequently transgressed the Sabbath rules
(Mk 2.25-26; Lk 6:3-4). But, far more important was the defence which
claimed that Jesus as Son of man had authority to determine the
Sabbath's laws and use (Mk 2:28; Mt 12:6).

(ii)   The driving out of evil spirits by Beelzebul. There was a general
belief in Jesus' day in demon possession. The demons aided the
Devil's opposition to God by harming humans; they were thought to
inhabit the air, lying in wait to attack men. It was also assumed that
false prophets were able to use sorcery to seduce the people. Such
were the presuppositions for the attack on Jesus: his enemies, unable
to deny his power, attributed it to the influence of Beelzebul, the
prince of the world of demons.

In Luke 11:20 there is a saying, generally considered authentic, where Jesus suggests that it is 'by the finger of God' that he casts out demons. Norman Perrin has pointed out that this expression can be found in the Exodus account of the plagues (*Ex* 8:19), i.e. the exorcisms, far from being the work of Beelzebul, are evidence of the functioning of God's Kingdom (*Mt* 12:28). Such being the case, men and women can now experience 'the new Exodus'.

(iii)   His association and table fellowship with ostracised people, 'sinners and tax collectors'. Time and again, the Gospels tell of how freely, and naturally, Jesus had contact with 'sinners and tax collectors'. That does not mean that the events must have taken place exactly as the texts indicate. Yet even if the accounts have been stylised, scholars consider that they have nonetheless 'a paradigmatic trustworthiness, an incontestable inner truth', i.e. 'they give us a faithful picture of Jesus and the people to whom he was devoted' (Aulén).

'Tax collectors and sinners' is a common combination in the Gospels. Both were regarded as outsiders by the pious Jew. Sinners were those who did not carefully observe the religious regulations and commandments. Indeed, the Jewish tradition made little or no distinction between moral and ritual requirements; all the commandments were alike considered to be the will of God. Tax collectors worked for the Roman occupation forces and were of two classes: there were the general tax officials who collected taxes on property and income, and the custom house officials who were responsible for the special taxes on, for example, the use of roads. Both were condemned by the rabbis for their unjust and cruel exactions, their petty tyranny and avarice, and they naturally incurred the dislike and hatred of all patriots among their fellow-countrymen. Jesus' table fellowship with these "pariahs of his world" (Geza Vermes) became a representation of the Kingdom; the Pharisees considered that such association delayed its coming (*Mt* 11:16-19).

(iv)   It is generally believed that, at the time of Jesus, the forgiveness of sins was seen as the prerogative of God alone. Mark records the reaction of the Jewish authorities who were immediately ready with their judgement: 'It is blasphemy! Who can forgive sins but God alone?' (*Mk* 2:7). Commenting on this, Aulén concludes that Jesus' claim to forgive sins must have been historically correct.

D. Jesus as trainer

The gospels present Jesus as one who trained disciples to continue his work. From the larger company of followers he chose twelve men to be especially with him, and whom he could send out to preach his message, cast out demons and heal the sick (*Mk* 3:14f). The urgency of the situation is seen in the instructions given to the disciples in *Mk* 6:7-13. Luke records the sending out of a much larger number on a separate occasion, suggesting that although these responsibilities were primarily delegated to the 'Twelve', they were not confined to them (*Lk* 10:1-16; see also, *Mk* 5:19, 9:38-41).

In every case, discipleship meant giving Jesus an exclusive loyalty whatever the cost (*Mk* 8:34-38; *LK* 14:26-33). In at least some cases it meant the literal abandonment of home, employment ties and possessions (*Mk* 10:21, 28). When Jesus gathered disciples around him in this way, he created a new community; a community 'which was an anticipation of that which was to come' (Aulén). Jeremias goes so far as to suggest that 'the only significance of the whole of Jesus' activity is to gather the eschatological people of God' (*New Testament Theology* p170).

CHAPTER THREE

JESUS: THE LAST WEEK IN JERUSALEM

All of the Gospels describe the last days culminating in Jesus' crucifixion with considerable detail. What is reported is considered to belong to the oldest layers of tradition. The four Gospel writers take up the tradition, but each gives it a particular interpretation in terms of his theology.

1. Mark's account

Jesus enters Jerusalem in humble fashion (11:1-10; see *Zech* 9.9). The cleansing of the Temple (11:15-19) is inserted into the story of the fig tree (11:12-14, 20-25). The cursing of the fig tree may have developed from the parable of Luke 13:6-9, where the unfruitful tree symbolises an unfaithful people (*Isa* 5:1-7; *Jer* 8.13; *Mic* 7.1) and, along with the expulsion of the buyers and sellers from the Temple, constitutes a parabolic action of the kind familiar in the prophets (e.g. *Jer* 27:2; *Ezek* 4:1-5.17). The sequel is a plot against the life of Jesus (11:18), for the moment frustrated because he is too popular. Jesus' act of challenge to the Temple authorities (the chief priests, scribes, and elders; i.e. the constituent parts of the Sanhedrin) is met by their challenge to him over the source of his authority (11:28-33). As often (e.g. 10:3, 12:16), Jesus answers with a counterquestion, asking them to take a stand on the baptism of John. The question leaves the deputation in a dilemma (11:31f), but carries a veiled claim that Jesus is the Messiah; like that of John, his authority is 'from God' (11:30).

Jesus reappears in the Temple (chap 12) and openly attacks his opponents. In the parable of the tenants in the vineyard he makes clear his repudiation of the current leadership in Israel (12:1-12). In its present form the parable manifests strong allegorical elements: the verbal similarity between 12:1 and *Isa* 5:1-2, where the vineyard represents Israel; the repeated sending of 'servants' (an O.T. term for prophets, *Jer* 7:25, 25:4; *Amos* 3:7; *Zech* 1:6) and their violent rejection (*1 Kings* 18:13, 22:26-27; *2 Chron* 24:20-22, 36:15-16); the final sending of the 'beloved son', a term used elsewhere for Jesus (*Mk* 1:11, 9:7);

and the destruction of the tenants and the transfer of the vineyard 'to others' (12:9). The story leads into a quotation from *Ps* 118: 'The stone which the builders rejected has become the head of the corner; this was the Lord's doing, and it is marvellous in our eyes.'

The three controversies following the parable are not localised and are initiated by the three principal groups of opponents in the Gospel: Pharisees and Herodians (12:13; cf.3:6), Sadducees (12:18), and a scribe (12:28):-

(i)   The Question of the Tribute Money: 12:13-17. The delegation begins with flattery (verse 14), but the trap is immediately sprung: "Is it lawful to pay taxes to Caesar, or not? Should we pay them, or should we not?" The pronouncement (verse 17) affirms that loyalty to the emperor need not be inconsistent with loyalty to God, and will have been of the utmost importance to the early Church confronted by authorities determined to test the attitude of Christians towards the state. The narrative notes that Jesus' opponents 'were amazed at him' (verse 17).

(ii)   The Question of the Resurrection: 12.18-27. In this controversy the mode of argument consists of text and countertext, all taken from the Pentateuch, since (unlike the Pharisees) the Sadducees held that it alone was binding, i.e. they rejected the oral interpretations of the Law developed among the common folk. Their objection to resurrection involved an extreme interpretation of the law of levirate marriage (*Dtr* 25:5); a law designed to secure the continuance of the family line. Jesus attacks their assumption that the future life is merely a continuation of the present: "When they rise from the dead, they neither marry nor are given in marriage, but are like angels in heaven" (verse 25). He then cites *Exodus* 3:6 (the revelation of God's name to Moses) to produce a positive argument: if God was revealed as a God of the living, their ancestors must be alive (verses 26-27).

(iii)   The Supreme Commandment: 12:28-34. The two-part command is given by Jesus in reply to a scribe's question about the 'head' under which the Law might be summarised. The question is not hostile; the issue is simply what principles Jesus will choose, not whether he can do so.

The explicit mention of the Temple (12:35) recalls the setting of 11:27. Jesus now takes up the initiative citing a scribal opinion that the Messiah is a Son of David, only to reject it: The Messiah is 'more than' a Son of David (verse 37). Jesus then proceeds to condemn the practice of the scribes whose religion is a sham (verses 38-40). Mark concludes this account of Jesus' teaching in Jerusalem with his commendation of the widow who throws everything she has into the Temple treasury (verses 41-44).

In chapter 13, Mark concludes the public ministry with a private address of Jesus to four of his disciples, Peter, James, John and Andrew. The scene shifts from the Temple court (verses 1-2) to the Mount of Olives (verse 3), associated by *Zechariah* 14:4 with the coming of the 'day of the Lord' and by popular expectation with the appearance of the Messiah. Similarities of theme link this section with the account of Jesus' death and resurrection. The purpose of the discourse is to prepare the disciples for future events: the pattern of Jesus' life is to be reproduced in them (e.g. they too will be persecuted). What they must do is to preach the gospel (verse 10), to stand firm (verse 13), and be vigilant (verses 35-36).

The Passion narrative proper begins in chapter 14 with the story of the woman's anointing of Jesus in the house of Simon the leper at Bethany (verses 3-9). The story is inserted between two plots (14:1, 10) to contrast two attitudes toward the suffering Jesus, betrayal or devotion. The woman's action may also point forward to Jesus' imminent death (in 16:1 the attempt to anoint his body is frustrated by his resurrection).

It is clear from the description Mark gives of the arrangements for the meal (14:12-17) that he interprets the Last Supper as a celebration of the Passover. Different elements are interwoven: the prediction of Judas' betrayal (14:17-21); the institution of the Lord's Supper (14:22-26); and the prediction of Peter's denial (14:27-31). The meal interprets the death of Jesus as a work of sacrifice with representative content – 'for many' (14:24).

In Gethsemane, Mark gives prominence to the human emotions of Jesus. He begins to be 'greatly distressed and troubled' (14:33), and is overwhelmed with sorrow to the point of death (verse 34). He shrinks from the prospect that lies before him, "Father, all things are possible to thee; remove this cup from me" (14:36). The only answer he receives to his prayer 'is the hard answer of events' (Cranfield). It begins with the failure of Peter and James and John to watch with him (14:37, 40, 41). The treachery of Judas fulfils the earlier prophecy of 14:18. Betrayal by a kiss, the customary greeting for a Rabbi from a disciple, underlines the evil of Judas (14:45). After Jesus is seized, his disciples all flee.

The trial before the high priest (14:53-65) contrasts true and false confessions. 'False witnesses' (14:56, 57; the charge that Jesus would destroy the Temple and rebuild it in three days) may stem from the tradition of the trial of the righteous sufferer (*Ps* 27:12; 35:11). Mark interprets 'false' as 'their testimony did not agree' (14:59; the agreement of two or three witnesses was required to sustain the charge, cf. *Num* 35:30; *Dtr* 17:6, 19:15). In 14:61 the high priest challenges Jesus with the question, "are you the Christ, the Son of the Blessed?" Jesus replies, "I am; and you will see the Son of man seated at the right hand of Power, and coming with the clouds of heaven". Note how 'Son of man' is substituted for *christos*. The words are echoes of Daniel 7:13, with a phrase ('sitting at the right hand of Power', i.e. God) from Psalm 110:1. Jesus' messianic role is here one of future vindication and authority, not present political power. The trial concludes with the story of the mockery. At the very moment when Jesus is condemned as a false prophet (14:65), his prophecy about Peter is being fulfilled (14:66-72).

At dawn, a formal meeting of the Sanhedrin confirms the decisions reached during the night and Jesus is taken before Pilate (15:1, Pilate was Procurator of Judaea from CE 25/26-36). Pilate's question to Jesus is "Are you the King of the Jews?" rather than "Are you the Son of the Blessed?" i.e. the Jewish authorities had resolved to proceed on the basis of the political aspect of Jesus' messianic claims. Jesus' response to Pilate is simply, "You have said so" (15:2), followed by silence when the charge is repeated.

Mark now recounts the choice between Barabbas and Jesus (15:6-15; there is no independent evidence for the custom of releasing a prisoner at Passover). The theme of rejection continues: the crowds who had earlier acclaimed Jesus (11:9) prefer Barabbas. Pilate bends to the will of the mob (stirred up by the chief priests) and sends Jesus to the cross, even though he sees no good reason for this (15:14-15). Taking up the claim of kingship, the soldiers clothe Jesus in purple, give him a crown of thorns and hail him as king of the Jews (15:17, 18). On Mark 15:19, see *Isa* 50:6: 'I gave my back to the smiters, and my cheeks to those who pulled out the beard; I hid not my face from shame and spitting'.

The theme of humiliation and unbelief continues in the crucifixion narrative (15:21-41). Jesus is physically unable to carry his cross (verse 21). He is crucified naked and his clothes are divided among his captors (verse 24). He is mocked by the bystanders, Temple officials, and even by the 'bandits' crucified with him (verses 29-32). His humiliation is complete.

The final three hours of Jesus's life are marked by apocalyptic imagery of the precreation darkness (15:33; cf. *Gen* 1:2). At the ninth hour, Jesus utters a loud cry, "My God, my God, why hast thou forsaken me?" (*Ps* 22:1). The curtain in the Temple separating the Holy of Holies from the Holy Place is torn in two (verse 38), i.e. the death of Jesus opens the way into the presence of God. The culmination of the Christology of the Gospel comes with the centurion's testimony, "Truly this man was the Son of God" (15:39; a confession which confirms the access that the Gentiles now have to God).

2. Matthew's account

In his account of the entry into Jerusalem (21.1-11), Matthew follows Mark, but he adds *Zech* 9:9 with the introductory words from *Isa* 62:11 to make explicit those quotations from the Old Testament that had influenced the tradition. Note how Matthew chooses to take the text literally; instead of an ass only, he has Jesus ride on a she-ass with her colt (21:7). Unlike Mark, the cleansing of the Temple is the climax of the entry and is associated with healings, thus strengthening the messianic note (21:12-14). The parable of the tenants in the vineyard (21:33-46) is prefaced and followed by a non-Marcan parable: the two sons (21:28-32) and the marriage feast (22:1-14). At 22:15 Matthew returns to Mark and presents the questions and answers between Jesus and his opponents but with important changes, e.g. he makes the raising of the tribute money a deliberate plot engineered by the Pharisees who 'took counsel how to entangle him in his talk'. The material assembled in chapter 23 expands the sayings in *Mk* 12:38-40 and much of it is found in *Lk* 11:37-52. In chapter 24 Matthew follows Mark's apocalyptic discourse closely, again with additons. Of particular importance are the additional parables in chapter 25: the ten maidens (1-13), the talents (14-30), and the sheep and the goats (31-46).

The Passion narrative proper begins in *Matthew* 26. The Evangelist follows Mark quite closely though he feels free to omit, to add, and to change details as he wishes. In 26.2 Jesus himself announces the approach of the Passover and adds a new Son of man prediction. In the account of Judas' betrayal (26:14-16), Matthew changes Mark's 'they promised to give him money' (*Mk* 14:11) to 'they paid him thirty pieces of silver' (verse 15). The words are a quotation from *Zech* 11:12. Scholars think it unlikely that Matthew had historical information about this point; rather has he read the detail out of the

Old Testament (see Fenton, p413). To the prediction of the betrayal
at the Last Supper, Matthew adds 26:25, in which Jesus names Judas
as the betrayer. In the trial before the Sanhedrin, the high priest
makes a further effort to secure a conviction, by putting Jesus under
oath (26:63). To the question whether he is the Christ, the Son of
God, Jesus replies not "I am", as in Mark, but, "You have said so"
(26:64; i.e. "the words are yours, not mine"). In the crucifixion scene
(27:33-44), Matthew adds that the wine offered to Jesus was mingled
with gall (verse 34), a detail taken from *Ps* 69:21. Matthew further
underlines the fulfilment of Scripture at 27:43, quoting *Ps* 22:8,
together with the explanation 'for he said, "I am the Son of God".'
This recalls the temptation story (*Mt* 4:3, 6) and so presents the
crucifixion as Jesus' last temptation. At the death of Jesus (27:50-54),
the centurion 'and those who were with him' declare: "Truly this
was the Son of God". In Matthew the declaration is not a confession
of faith, but an expression of fear at the supernatural events taking
place.

We should note also six major insertions into the Passion narrative:
26:52-54, 27:3-10, 27:19, 27:24-25, 27:51b-53, 27:62-66.

3. Luke's account

The entrance of Jesus into Jerusalem is given much as in Mark, with
some variations and additions (19:28-44). Luke alone pictures the
descent from the Mount of Olives and he identifies the crowds as
disciples (verse 37). In verses 43-44 the destruction of Jerusalem is
predicted; the siege imagery may be based on the Old Testament (*Isa*
29:3, 37:33; *Jer* 52:4-5; *Ezek* 4:1-3), though scholars also point out that
the siege is exactly predicted, i.e. this could have been written after
the event. Luke greatly abbreviates Mark's account of the cleansing
of the Temple (19:45-48). The Temple is cleansed for Jesus' ministry
of teaching the people (verse 47). In the parable of the tenants in the
vineyard (20:9-18) only the son is killed, and that is done 'outside'
(verse 15), so as to correspond with the actual death of Jesus outside
Jerusalem. The question about the greatest commandment is dealt
with earlier on in the Gospel at 10:25-28. The apocalyptic discourse
(21:5-38) is a modified form of Mark 13. Note how Jesus speaks in the
Temple (verses 5-7, 37-38) and not from the Mount of Olives (*Mk*
13.3). Luke's view of the Temple is a positive one in both the Gospel
and Acts. Luke provides his own ending to the discourse (verses
34-36), omitting Mark's parable of a man going on a journey (*Mk*
13:34). This passage may well owe a great deal to *Isa* 24:17ff.

The Passion narrative proper begins in chapter 22. In 22:1-2 Luke abbreviates Mark, omitting 'not during the feast' (*Mk* 14.2) as inconsistent with what follows. At 22:3 the action of Judas is attributed to Satan, i.e. the sufferings and death of Jesus constitute a battleground between God and the forces of evil. Mark's story of the anointing of Jesus (14:3-9) is deleted here and placed elsewhere (*Lk* 7:36-50; it is recast as the loving response of a forgiven sinner). Luke identifies Peter and John as the disciples sent to prepare the Passover (22:8). The arrangements recall the preparation for the entry into Jerusalem at 19:28-34. Luke frames Jesus' words at the Last Supper (22:14-38) as a farewell by a leader to his followers: first the meal (verses 14-20), and then Jesus' teaching on what will happen and how the disciples are to conduct themselves (verses 21-38). Unlike Mark, the prophecy of betrayal does not overshadow the words of institution (22:21-23; cp. *Mk* 14:17-21). Peter's denial of Jesus is mollified by the promise of his future important role (22:31-34). In the account of Gethsemane (22:39-53), Luke softens Mark's rebuke of the disciples and explains their sleep as due to sorrow (verse 45). Note, too, that the disciples' desertion of Jesus is not described (cp. *Mk* 14:50). Peter's denial takes place before any trial begins and the scene carries more pathos in Luke: 'And the Lord turned and looked at Peter' (22:61). In the trial before Pilate there is an insertion of a trial before Herod which provides Luke with a further opportunity of exculpating the governor (23:6-16). Luke records the sympathy of the women (23:27), of the penitent thief (23:39-43), and of the crowds (23:48), and has no reference to the cry of dereliction (*Mk* 15:34). Jesus prays, "Father, forgive them; for they know not what they do" (23:34). In the person of the centurion (23:47), Rome again declares Jesus' innocence.

4. John's account

The entry into Jerusalem is recorded in 12:12-19. The account is similar to the Synoptics', particularly in the crowd's greeting (cp. *Mt* 21.5 on the use of *Zech* 9:9; *Lk* 19:38 for Jesus hailed as King). Unlike Mark, John places the finding of the ass after the crowd's ovation (verse 14); his intention may have been 'to show that Jesus could and would accept the designation King (6:15) only when this was defined in terms of Zechariah's Prince of Peace, who rides not on a warhorse but on an ass' (Barrett). John's distinctive theology is seen in verse 16, with the note that the disciples did not understand the event until after Jesus's glorification (cp. 2:17, 22). John records the despair of the Pharisees (verse 19): "You see that you can do nothing; look, the world has gone after him." Ironically, the words 'suggest Jesus' mission to, and salvation of, the world.' (Barrett)

The Temple cleansing, which comes next in the Synoptics, has occurred much earlier in John (2:13-25; it is the opening event in Jesus' Jerusalem ministry). Here we have evidence of the Evangelists' creative reconstruction. Marsh observes that for John, 'The story of the Passion and Crucifixion did not begin just a week before Christ died; his whole life was passion and crucifixion.' The narrative begins in a manner similar to the other Gospels, although there are differences in detail: Jesus' use of a whip (verse 15); his direct address to the vendors of pigeons (verse 16). Only in John does Jesus say, "you shall not make my Father's house a house of trade" (verse 16). The quotation of *Ps* 69:9 (at verse 17) has a two-fold significance; it refers to the zeal that motivated Jesus' deed, and it alludes to his own death (Barrett notes that the Psalmist traces his own suffering to his zeal for the Temple). Jesus' saying in verse 19 ("Destroy this temple, and in three days I will raise it up") is, in Mark, attributed to Jesus by his opponents and does not occur in this setting (*Mk* 14:58; 15:29). The question of the Jews (verse 20) enables the Evangelist to inform his readers of the real meaning of Jesus' words (verse 21) and to point ahead to the disciples' future belief (verse 22).

Again, it is significant that, in comparison with Mark, John reverses the order of the anointing (12:1-8) and the entry (12:12-19). Here in the Fourth Gospel, Jesus enters the capital as its anointed king. Note the points of resemblance to both the Marcan (14:3-9) and the Lucan (7:36-50) stories.

The incident with the Greeks (12:20-36) is important because it seems to end Christ's public ministry in John. The 'Greeks' referred to here are probably non-Jews who represent the Gentile world from which, when John wrote, the majority of Christians were drawn. In response to their request Jesus speaks to the crowd around him (verses 23f.). The time has now come, he implies, for him to act rather than to speak; his death and resurrection will speak for themselves to the entire Gentile world. Note the fear Jesus feels as he comtemplates the ordeal of his death (verses 27f.), evoking the Gethsemane scene of the synoptic Gospels (*Mk* 14:32-42 and parallels), otherwise not mentioned in John.

The public ministry over, Jesus takes supper with his disciples on Passover eve (13:1-30). According to the Synoptics, the meal was the Passover itself (*Mk* 14:12, 16, 17, etc.). Each of these datings may be theologically motivated, whether it be that the Eucharist is to be represented as the Passover meal (Synoptics) or whether Jesus himself is to be shown as the true Passover lamb, who died at the hour when the lambs were slaughtered (John; see *Jn* 1.29 for the identification of Jesus with the lamb of God). The narrative contains material closely parallel to the synoptic accounts, i.e. the fact that a supper was taken on the last night of Jesus' life, and the prediction of Judas' betrayal (verses 21-30). On the other hand, John omits Jesus' institution of the Eucharist (the synoptic words in explanation of the bread and the wine), and includes the narrative of Jesus' washing of the disciples' feet (verses 4-11), which is reported in no other Gospel.

At 13:31-38 we move from the narrative of the supper to the farewell discourses of chps. 14-16 and the prayer of Jesus in chp. 17. The distinctiveness of these chapters is obvious in relation to the synoptic accounts. Even so, they afford a partial parallel to the apocalyptic discourse of *Mark* 13 in that they tell the disciples what they may expect in the future.

The Passion narrative proper begins in chapter 18 with the account of Jesus' arrest (verses 1-11). There are fairly close parallels in the Synoptics (e.g. *Mk* 14:43-50) but with important differences. John does not describe Jesus' agony nor the flight of the disciples. Throughout the emphasis is on the authority of Jesus: he goes out voluntarily to his arrest (verses 4, 5); his mere speech is sufficient to repel his adversaries (verse 6); he preserves his disciples at the cost of himself (verse 8; interpreted in verse 9 as the fulfilment of Jesus' earlier word, see 6:39). John does not describe a trial before the Sanhedrin, and he is the only one to report the interrogation before Annas (18:13, 19-24). The relation between Annas and Caiaphas (18:13) is not mentioned elsewhere. Despite himself, Caiaphas tells us the significance of the passion: Jesus is dying for all the people (18:14).

The principal scene in John's passion is the Roman trial (18:28 – 19:16). The fundamental points in the story are shared by John with Mark: the examination of Jesus before Pilate, Pilate's unwillingness to condemn Jesus, the reference to Barabbas and to the custom of releasing one prisoner at Passover, the scourging, the mockery, the clamour for the death of Jesus, and the handing over for crucifixion. The comings and goings of Pilate, from Jesus who is inside the praetorium to the Jews who refuse to enter, break up the episode into seven scenes, with the crowning of Jesus with thorns at their centre. Jesus' counter-questioning of Pilate, and Pilate's rejoinder, are unique to John (18:34-35), as is Jesus' statement, "My kingship is not of this world" (18:36). The scene ends with Pilate, in spite of all appearances, truly proclaiming Jesus king (19:14).

It is as king that Jesus is crucified: the inscription bears this out (19:20). Only in John do we read that the title was written in Hebrew, in Latin, and in Greek (19:20), and that the chief priests wanted it changed to indicate that Jesus only claimed to be king of the Jews (19:21). There is no mocking of Jesus on the cross (*Mk* 15:29-32); no cry of dereliction (*Mk* 15:34); no tearing of the veil of the Temple at Jesus' death (*Mk* 15:38); and no word from the centurion (*Mk* 15:39). Jesus' thirsting (*Jn* 19:28) allows Scripture to be fulfilled (*Ps* 69:21); as in *Mark* (15:36) he is given vinegar to drink (19:29). In *John*, Jesus says simply, "It is finished", and gives up his spirit (19:30; i.e. sends out his Spirit into the world). The final scene, the piercing of Jesus' side (19:31-37), appears only in *John*. The fact that no bone of Jesus is broken (verse 33) is the fulfilment of prophecy (verse 36). The reference may be to *Exodus* 12:46 or *Numbers* 9:12 both of which refer to the Passover lamb, i.e. Jesus dies as the true Passover. The spear-thrust (verse 34) also fulfils prophecy (verse 37; see *Zech* 12:10, which speaks of the mourning of Jerusalem for him whom they have pierced), but John further notes that the spear-thrust results in the effusion of blood and water. The blood and water came to have symbolic value for Christians as signifying the Eucharist and baptism, whether or not that meaning was understood or intended by John. Barrett observes, 'These sacraments find their meaning only in the death of Jesus which is the life of men.'

Resurrection appearances

Did Jesus' crucifixion render his life and ministry meaningless? Did he enter into the past as a failure and in this sense become the 'historical' Jesus? According to the New Testament documents, his disciples were given the answer soon after his death through various resurrection appearances (*1 Cor* 15:3-8) and the experience of his presence in the Spirit. The faith of the primitive church grew out of this.

The first important question to ask here is: are the accounts of Jesus' resurrection based on historical fact? There are several difficulties and inconsistencies in the texts: a solid body (*Lk* 24:36-43) with real wounds (*Jn* 20:24-29) that can pass through walls (*Jn* 20:19); a body that is recognisable (*Mt* 28:9 and *Lk* 24:36-38) or unrecognisable (*Lk* 24:16 and *Jn* 20:14); appearances take place in Galilee only (*Matthew* and *John* chapter 21), or in Jerusalem only (*Luke* and *John* chapter 20). As with all the gospel material, each of the four evangelists selects and shapes the story in such a way as to emphasise his particular view of the truth about Jesus. In reality there is nothing by way of external or objective evidence. That which is directly accessible to scholarship is only the existence of groups of people, in first-century Palestine and beyond, all convinced of the aliveness of the man, Jesus of Nazareth, who had been put to death by crucifixion.

Because the disciples were convinced of the identity of the Risen One with the earthly Jesus, they applied christological titles of honour to him. Among these 'Messiah' was of especial importance. The Gospels consistently show Jesus' reluctance to accept the title without qualification (e.g. *Mk* 8:27-33) because 'messiah' popularly referred to a king in the line of David, the conqueror of the heathen, the saviour and restorer of Israel, all of which was outside Jesus' own understanding of his mission. But after Jesus' death the risk of misunderstanding no longer existed. 'Messiah' took on a specifically Christian meaning as 'messiaship' was restricted in the Church to Jesus' sacrificial act on the cross. The messiah Jesus is the crucified agent of God who had died 'for our sins' (*1 Cor* 15:3). With the mission to the Gentiles a further development took place as the Greek equivalent *Christos* became a proper name: Jesus Christ.

An important Old Testament text to be applied to Jesus was *Psalm* 110:1, 'The Lord says to my lord: "Sit at my right hand, till I make your enemies your footstool"'. Here the word 'Lord' is used both for God and the messianic king. During his earthly ministry, Jesus had been addressed as, 'my Lord', in recognition of his unusual authority (*Mt* 7:21; the Aramaic word, *mari*, did not imply divinity). But the application of *Psalm* 110:1 to Jesus meant that the title 'My Lord' implied that he was the Messiah. Hence we get the liturgical acclamation in Aramaic *marana tha*, "Our Lord, come" (*1 Cor* 16:22; *Rev* 22:20).

Christian belief in Jesus as Son of God appears to be rooted in *Psalm* 2:7, 'I will tell of the decree of the Lord: He said to me, "You are my son, today I have begotten you." In this coronation psalm, the king is given a sonship of higher order than the children of Israel in general (cp. *Hosea* 11:1, where the term is predicated of Israel constitued as a nation through the Exodus). At his resurrection, Jesus is "designated Son of God in power according to the Spirit of holiness" (*Rom* 1:4), i.e. he embarks "upon a new role in salvation history as the mediator of God's final offer of salvation" (R.H. Fuller).

The New Testament expands this Christology even further. In the Prologue to the Fourth Gospel (1:1-18), Christ is the Word (*Logos*; a frequent word in the Greek Old Testament denoting 'God in action'). The Word did not come into being but 'was'; and was with God, and participated in God's being (verse 1). The Word was active in all aspects of Creation (verse 3; cp. *Gen* 1:3); the source of life and light for humanity (verse 4). The Word 'became flesh' (verse 14), incarnate in Jesus Christ.

According to *Philippians* 2:5-11, the pre-existent Christ 'in the form of God', was 'born in the likeness of men' and 'humbled himself', and was consequently 'highly exalted' by God, with a view to the entire created order yielding him at the last reverence as sovereign Lord: 'that at the name of Jesus every knee should bow, in heaven and on earth and under the earth, and every tongue confess that Jesus Christ is Lord, to the glory of the God the Father (verses 10-11).

To this Christological development belong finally the birth narratives of Matthew and Luke. In both accounts the title 'Son of God' is moved back to the conception of Jesus (*Mt* 1:20; *Lk* 1:35), emphasising the messianic role that the child is destined to play in salvation history. Jesus, already in the womb, is the chosen one, the Son of the Most High.

CHAPTER FOUR

THE BREAK WITH JUDAISM

That which ultimately emerged as normative Christianity was
originally but one among various contending Christian groups. *The
Acts of the Apostles*, the only account of early Jerusalem Christianity
we possess, records how the 'Gentile Christian' trend won out and
the Pauline approach became accepted as expressing the way
forward for the Church. Because Acts is a theological narrative (chp
1), it would be unwise to consult the work uncritically as if one might
abstract from it pure historical facts. A source against which we can
check some of what is recorded in Acts is the writings of Paul. In his
letters, Paul notes the antagonisms and conflicts that hindered his
easy contact with Gentiles: *Philippians* 3, *2 Corinthians* 11, *Romans* 9,
and *Galtians* 2 and 3. These chapters show that the early Christians
were not so 'unified in spirit' (J.D.G. Dunn) as *Acts* portrays; note, in
particular, the tendency to make Peter and Paul alike in regard to
Gentile freedom and the Law (cf. *Gal* 2:11-14). A striking set of
parallel accounts for Peter and Paul suggest an intention to equalise
the two apostles: 3:2 and 14:8; 5:5 and 13:11; 5:15 and 19:12; 5:17, 34
and 23:6, 9; 8:20 and 13:10; 9:34 and 28:8; 9:40 and 20:10; 10:1 and
13:12; 10:20 and 22:17; 10:26 and 16:29; 10:44 and 19:6; 12:7 and 16:26.
It would appear that the author of *Acts* viewed the early Christians as
models for conduct and that he has attempted to smooth out the
differences in the early Church.

The Jewish-Christian Community in Jerusalem

For some years after Jesus, his disciples remained one of the many
sub-groups within Judaism. They took part in the regular worship of
the Temple, observed the festivals and in general kept the Law of
Moses. Their distinctive feature lay in their proclamation that the
Messiah had come, had been resurrected from death, and would
return to usher in the Messianic Age. But, as David Christie-Murray
says, 'The doctrine was unorthodox rather than heretical; it did not
strike at the roots of Judaism' (*A History of Heresy*, p 13). In fact, the
apostles appear to have been held in high regard by the Jerusalem

populace (*Acts* 2:47) and among their converts counted priests (*Acts* 6:7) and members of the Pharisees (*Acts* 15:5). It is likely that many of the Pharisaic party regarded these Aramaic-speaking Judaeo-Christians (the 'Hebrews') with respect, because of their godly and righteous living. *Acts* records that when Peter and John were arrested and brought before the Sanhedrin, for proclaiming Jesus as Messiah and working miracles in his name, it was a leader of the Pharisees, Gamaliel, who interceded on their behalf (*Acts* 5:34-40).

Stephen

For the author of *Acts* 7, Stephen's speech recorded in *Acts* provides the justification for turning to the Gentiles. *Acts* is a book which proclaims the *Gospel* through the speeches and deeds of the early Christians and through the way in which Gospel types recur: for example, the martyrdom of Stephen who suffers under the same charge as Jesus, and makes the same prayers. *Acts* 6 informs us that Stephen belonged to the group of 'Hellenisers'; that is, Christian Jews (or proselytes) who spoke Greek and who tended to adopt a freer life-style than the more conservative 'Hebrews'. Stephen was scathing of the worship carried out in the Temple. He soon fell foul of the crowd and was brought before the Sanhedrin on the charge of saying that "this Jesus of Nazareth will destroy this place, and will change the customs which Moses delivered to us" (*Acts* 6:9-14).

The report of his defence before the Sanhedrin may well represent the general direction of Stephen's teaching:-

1   He revered the Law of Moses ('living oracles'; *Acts* 7:38); but the building of the Temple was an act of idolatry, God's presence cannot be localised, 'the Most High does not dwell in houses made with hands' (*Acts* 7:48).

2   Moses had predicted that 'God will raise up for you a prophet from your brethren' as he had raised up Moses (*Acts* 7:37). In killing Christ, the Jewish leaders had resisted the Holy Spirit (*Acts* 7:51); they stood in the line of those who had slain the prophets (*Acts* 7:52); they were now apostates from the Law (*Acts* 7:53; 'you who received the law as delivered by angels and did not keep it').

Stephen's words infuriated the council; when he claimed to see the 'Son of Man standing at the right hand of God' (as his advocate?) he was seized and stoned to death (*Acts* 7:54f). We are told that a wave of persecution now followed. The Hellenisers within the Church fled Jerusalem to the Diaspora, taking the message into the Diaspora synagogues and soon afterwards to the Gentiles (*Acts* 11:19f). It seems that the Judaeo-Christians who remained behind, carefully observed the Law in order to be able to live and work further among Israel.

Philip the Evangelist

According to *Acts*, the refugees of the Hellenistic party went far and wide. Philip preached in Samaria, a district in which a by-form of Judaism existed alongside various pagan cults. Here he encountered Simon Magus (Simon The Magician, or The Sorcerer), a successful and famous practitioner of magical arts who cultivated the belief that he was a divine emanation, 'that power of God which is called Great' (*Acts* 8:10). Simon attended Philip's preaching, professed belief in Christ and was baptised. He was soon expelled from the Church after offering to purchase from the apostles Peter and John the supernatural power of transmitting the Holy Spirit, i.e. he thought it resided in the apostles themselves as super-magicians. Peter and John had been sent to supervise Philip's work, since each stage in the development of the Christian mission had to be accepted by the Jerusalem Church. It is significant that the converts in Samaria were the first to receive the gift of the Holy Spirit by the laying on of hands with prayer (*Acts* 8:15,17). Philip did not lay on hands, possibly because his authority was limited. The admission of the Samaritans raised various problems. It is true that they were already circumcised and did in some sense keep the Law; they accepted only the Pentateuch (the first five books of the Old Testament). But could they be permitted to go on worshipping in their own Temple on Gerizim, as the Jewish Christians did in the Temple at Jerusalem? In any case, they could not worship at Jerusalem.

A vivid and dramatic story now describes how Philip was sent south to the Jerusalem-Gaza road to lead the Ethiopian eunuch to Christ (*Acts* 8:26-39). This man was in touch with Judaism; he may even have been a Jewish convert. However, because of his emasculation, he was outside the covenant and forbidden by the Law to enter the congregation (*Lev* 21:20; *Deut* 23:21). But, he had come to faith in Christ, and on the basis of his faith Philip could not deny him baptism: 'And as they went along the road they came to some water, and the eunuch said, "See, here is water!: What is to prevent my being baptised?" . . . And he commanded the chariot to stop, and they both went down into the water, Philip and the eunuch, and he baptised him' (*Acts* 8:36, 38; some ancient authorities include all or most of verse 37, 'And Philip said, "If you believe with all your heart, you may". And he replied, "I believe that Jesus Christ is the Son of God.").'

After this incident *Acts* tells that Philip went to Azotus, and from there conducted an itinerant ministry until he reached Caesarea (*Acts* 8:40), where he seems to have remained (*Acts* 21:8).

The Church at Antioch

Others of the refugees travelled to Phoenicia, the island of Cyprus and to Antioch in Syria, the third city of the Empire and one time capital of the Seleucid Kingdom. It was in the metropolis of Antioch that we are told that the step of preaching direct to Gentiles was first taken (*Acts* 11:20). Acts tells that the message of Jesus was preached with such success there that "a great number that believed turned to the Lord" (11:21). In 'turning to the Lord' we are meant to include repentance and baptism (*Acts* 2:38) but not circumcision. *Acts* 15:1 and *Galatians* 2:11-14 show that these Gentile Christians were not circumcised. Nor was there any obligation to the Law on the part of those who believed (*Gal* 2:21), although they will have observed the central commandments (*Mark* 10:18f.; 12:28f.).

It is likely that large numbers of Gentile converts came from a group on the fringe of Judaism known as *Yereim* or *Yirei adonai* ('God-fearers'; Cornelius was one such, *Acts* 10:2). From the second century BCE the Jews had been actively proselytising. The God-fearers had abandoned polytheism and idolatry, accepted monotheism and the moral code of Judaism, but were unwilling to accept the full Torah observance. They were not circumcised and did not observe the Sabbath or the dietary laws; therefore, they were not accepted fully into Jewish communion, i.e. they could not marry Jews and did not count for a *minyan* (the congregational quorum of ten males). Christianity was obviously attractive to the God-fearers: it would admit them as full members without circumcision, and it did not require them to submit to the Mosaic Law. When Christian preachers appeared they went over in large numbers to the new teaching. Indeed, Dr. Solomon Goldman states that, 'The foundations of a Gentile Christian Church were laid almost exclusively among these proselytes, or among people already interested in Judaism' (*Facing*

Realities, p19). He quotes James Parkes, 'The transition by which these groups passed from partial membership of Judaism to full membership of the Christian Church was an easy one . . . What Christianity offered them was not something completely different but the same thing with, in addition, the power of Jesus Christ in place of the disadvantages of circumcision and other ritual prescriptions'.

Certainly, the crowd of Antioch did not recognise the new converts as Jews. For they soon gave them the nickname 'Christians' which quickly spread as the popular name. It was accepted as a title of honour (= 'followers of a leader Christ').

The growth of the new community soon drew to itself the attention of the Mother-Church at Jerusalem, who sent down Barnabas to investigate. 'A good man, full of the Holy Spirit and of faith', his approbation and encouragement significantly increased the number of converts (*Acts* 11:24). It was Barnabas who recognised the Chruch at Antioch as a fitting sphere of work for Paul, whom he brought to the city to share his ministry (*Acts* 11:25-26). Under their direction, what had begun as 'spontaneous enterprise' became 'a determined mission' (Eric Franklin, *Christ the Lord*, p129). The new community acknowledged its fellowship with the Jerusalem Church by sending relief to the poor there (*Acts* 11:29-30).

Conflict

At Antioch the admission of Gentile converts had created a mixed congregation, in which the Jewish members were prepared to forego the 'Laws pertaining to things clean and unclean' for the sake of Christian fellowship. In the Mother-Church, however, many Christians opposed this liberal attitude, maintaining that Gentile converts should be required to accept circumcision and the obligations of Torah. Their opposition is understandable. Any action which could be counted against the Church by the Jewish authorities was bound to have an extremely damaging effect on the Church's mission in Judaea. How could Christian Jews expect to go on communicating with non-Christian Jews, if they were thought to be on intimate terms with Gentiles? It is interesting that Dr. Dodd connects Herod's persecution of the apostles with Peter's reception of the Gentile Cornelius into full fellowship with the Church (*Acts* 10:44-48): Herod put to death James, the son of Zebedee, and imprisoned Peter with the intention of killing him (*Acts* 12:1-4; see

C.H.Dodd in *A Companion to the Bible*, p396). Leadership in the Jerusalem Church then fell to James, the Lord's brother, and the most orthodox of the Judaeo-Christians (*Acts* 12:17; 15:13; 21:18).

As a result of the first missionary journey of Barnabas and Paul (to Asia Minor; *Acts* 13,14), the rift in the Church between Hellenisers and Judaisers grew ever deeper. Barnabas and Paul had admitted numerous Gentiles into the Church without circumcision and subjection to Torah, and in some places entire congregations may have been composed solely of Gentiles. There was now a real danger that the continuity of the covenantal community was being lost. For the author of Acts, the problem is resolved by the authoritative decision of the Mother-Church (*Acts* 15).

The Council of Jerusalem

On the return of Barnabas and Paul to Antioch, emissaries from the Jerusalem Church, anxious that the Gentile mission should be put at once on a satisfactory basis, raised the whole question of the relation of converts from paganism to the Jewish Law. Christian Pharisees argued that since the Christian Church was the direct heir of ancient Israel, converts must be required to become Jews first, and so through the Jewish communion enter the Christian Church. In other words, they must submit themselves to circumcision and accept the ceremonial regulations of the Mosaic Law. Antioch took a different view. According to *Acts*, Paul and Barnabas went up to Jerusalem and the matter was discussed.

Acts tells how the apostle Peter was throughout on the side of the freedom of the Gentiles. Though not mentioning Cornelius by name, he recalled how he himself had been chosen by God to evangelise the Gentiles (*Acts* 15:7). When these received the Holy Spirit their hearts were purified and they believed. If one Gentile was accepted by God on faith alone, why not others? The conference had no right to impose the 'yoke' of the Law upon the uncircumcised whom God was calling (see *Acts* 15:10). Peter's arguments were continued by those of Barnabas and Paul who recounted the signs and miracles worked by God through them among the Gentiles. In the event, James ranged himself with Paul and so decided the issue. The Decree was that Gentile converts should "abstain from the pollutions of idols and from unchastity and from what is strangled and from blood" (*Acts* 15:20). The aim seems to have been to forbid practices which would prevent Jewish and Gentile Christians from sharing the common meals of the Church and to demand a standard of conduct worthy of the followers of Jesus. Yet what was far more important than the prohibitions was the lack of demand for circumcision and allegiance to the full Torah. Here was a great ground for divergence. As Dr. Goldman says, "The ruling created Jews whom the Rabbinate could not accept as Jews. It opened the door to the Church becoming increasingly, and ultimately predominantly, a Church of Gentiles."

In recent years the historicity of the Council has been sharply questioned, especially in relation to the evidence of Paul who never mentions the Decree in his writings. The problem partly turns on the relation of the visits of Paul to Jerusalem described in *Galatians* and those described in *Acts*. It is generally agreed that the first visit in *Galatians* (1:18-24) corresponds to the first in *Acts* (9:26-30). The traditional view equates the second visit described in *Galatians* (2:1-10) with the visit for the Jerusalem Council (*Acts* 15), which is the *third* visit recorded in Acts. If this identification is correct, the Epistle need not be later than the Council if the author of *Acts* is viewed as representing the Jerusalem account of the matter while Paul gives his own personal defence, i.e. the differences reflect the writers' standpoints. It is, however, held by many scholars that this identification is wrong and that the second visit of *Galatians* corresponds to the second visit in *Acts*, the famine visit (*Acts* 11). If this is right, the Apostolic Council has not yet taken place. The difficulty with this view is that it is plain that the author of *Acts* has omitted much in his narrative in chapter 11. There are two other possibilities:

(a)   that the narrative of *Acts* is confused and that *Acts* 11 and *Acts* 15 are two accounts of one and the same visit which is also described in *Gal* 2; or

(b)   that the visit described in *Gal* 2 is not to be equated with either of the visits in *Acts* 11 and 15.

The Final Breach

The next important turning-point in the divergence of Christianity from Judaism was the Roman-Jewish war of 66-70 CE. Eusebius (*Historia Ecclesiastica*, 3:5, 4) tells of the flight of the Judaeo-Christians to Pella in Transjordan, shortly before the destruction of Jerusalem; a tradition which could well indicate that high tension already existed between the Jews who were fighting for their independence and the deserting Christians. The lesson which the Judaeo-Christians drew from the fall of the city and the loss of the Temple and sacrificial worship strained relations with the rabbis to breaking-point (a number believed that Jesus had replaced sacrifice with baptism, annulling the precepts on sacrifice in the Pentateuch). They saw in the destruction the 'final departure of the sceptre from Israel' and taught that they, the disciples of Jesus, were now the true heirs of the promises of Israel.

To the Jews, *Torah* alone was left as the bond of religious and national identity. Dr. Goldman suggests that, 'had the Judaeo-Christians been the only members of the new faith, the breach between them and the Jews might have been healed, for they also desired to observe the Torah.' But the rabbis at Jamnia knew of their contact with Gentile Christians who did not submit themselves to circumcision and accept the ceremonial regulations of the Law. They were certainly aware of the teaching of Paul and condemned it. In Goldman's words, 'It was only a step from this condemnation to the refusal to accept as orthodox the conformity of the Judaeo-Christians.'

The step was taken when Samuel the Small (c80-100 CE), at the invitation of Gamaliel 11 of Jamnia, composed the 'benediction against the heretics' (*Birkat ha-minim*), included in the weekday Amidah prayer as the twelfth benediction. The declaration was so worded that the Judaeo-Christians might not pronounce it. The intention was either to keep the Judaeo-Christians out of the synagogues or to proclaim a definite breach between the two faiths. In any event, from that time onwards, Christians, whether Jew or Gentile, could not worship together with other Jews.

CHAPTER FIVE

CONFRONTATION WITH GNOSTICISM

Derived from the Greek word for knowledge, *gnosis*, the term
'Gnosticism' designates a number of philosophical and religious
systems that developed in the religious pluralism of the Hellenistic
world and flourished from the second to the fifth centuries CE. The
systems were philosophical in that the problem with which they
concerned themselves was how to reconcile the existence of evil with
God who is good. They were religious in that they offered disciples
salvation. Gnosticism proved a serious threat to the Church as it
went out into the Hellenistic world.

Origins

It is difficult to pinpoint accurately the origins of Gnosticism.
Scholars point to the similarities between Gnostic thinking and the
Greek philosophical tradition of Plato and his followers. A different
origin has been sought in the ancient religion of Zoroastrianism.
Scholars believe that Judaism too made an important contribution to
the conceptions and the developments of Gnosticism.

1. Philosophical Dualism

Plato and his followers contrasted this imperfect, material world, of
sense and everyday experience, with a purer world of spirit. Spirit is
the unchanging and eternal principle, transcending and wholly
independent of, the world of sensible objects. Applied to the
understanding of the nature of man, this meant that man was
composed of a lower, material part (the body), and a higher, spiritual
part (the soul). Man's soul is immortal, it exists prior to the body, its
material prison-house, and it will go on existing after the body's
extinction. This kind of thinking often led to a radically ascetic
attitude towards sex and a general contempt for the body and for the
things of 'this world'. Plato believed that it was necessary to
suppress bodily desires so that the soul could be free to search for
knowledge and liberate itself from the hold of the body. Having

purified itself of bodily passions it would be worthy to return to its
spiritual home.

2. Religious Dualism

The theory that there are two gods that control the world, one of
light and goodness, the other of darkness and evil. This form of
dualism is expressed most characteristically in Zoroastrianism.
Zoroaster (6th century BCE) traced the origin of evil to an exercise of
free will at the beginning of creation, when the twin sons of the
divinity Ahura Mazda (the Wise Lord) entered into an eternal
conflict. One, Spenta Mainyu (Beneficent Spirit), chose to do good,
and acquired the attributes of truth, justice, and life. The other,
Angra Mainyu (Destructive Spirit), chose to do evil, thus bringing
misery, illness, and death into the world. According to Zoroaster,
the world would soon be consumed in a mighty conflagration from
which only the followers of the good would rise to share a new creation.

3. Jewish Motifs

One way in which Jewish motifs were infused into Gnosticism was
through the Hebrew Bible. Particular importance was attached to the
Fall (*Genesis* 3) which is interpreted as the downfall of the divine
principle into the material world. Their negative attitude toward the
world of natural existence led all Gnostics to view the God of Israel,
the Creator-Lawgiver, as an inferior god, and they strongly rejected
his Law. The Gnostic movement may also owe a great deal to Jewish
mystical speculations.

Most scholars hold the Essenes to be identical with the 'Dead Sea' or
'Qumran' sect, whose writings were found near Jericho from 1947
onwards. Dr. David Flusser has pointed out that, 'Common to both
gnosticism and the Dead Sea Scrolls is the view of esoteric
"knowledge" as a redemptive factor, which enables a group of select
people to bridge the abyss separating the human from the divine,
and to rise "from a spirit perverse to an understanding of you and to
stand in one company before you with the everlasting host and the
spirits of knowledge, to be renewed with all things that are and with
those versed in song together" (*Thanksgiving Psalms*, Cave 1,
Qumran, 11:13-14), and to be those "who heard the glorious voice
and saw the holy angels, men whose ears are opened and hear deep
things" (*War Scroll*, Cave 1, Qumran, 10:11).' He continues, 'The
literature of the sect also reflects a dualistic outlook on the world
conceiving a schism between the principle of good (the light) and the
principle of evil (the darkness) each with its own host of angels and

spirits.' But, this view, 'in contrast to its expression in gnosticism, does not step beyond the framework of Jewish belief in divine unity,' nor does it culminate 'in the notion of distinction between matter *per se* and the divine spiritual world' (D. Flusser, 'Gnosticism' in *Encyclopaedia Judaica*, vol.7, p638).

We should also note the contribution of Philo of Alexandria (c.BCE 20 – c.CE 50) who interpreted Judaism in terms of Hellenistic mystical philosophy. Philo persuaded himself that the teachings of Plato were contained in the Torah. The method by which the harmony was brought about is known as the allegorical method of interpreting Scripture, i.e. the text is treated as a code to be deciphered. For example, when the Book of Genesis tells us that Abraham sent away his wife's handmaiden, Hagar, this is not a particularly edifying piece of information. Philo consequently understood it to mean that the ideal man, represented by Abraham, has to send away his lust for material possessions or bodily pleasures (represented by Hagar) in order to follow the way of the mind (the example is given in Dr. Louis Jacobs', *Jewish Ethics, Philosophy and Mysticism*, p54). With Philo, God was the transcendent Being, outside and above the world, so far removed that in order to relate him to the cosmos all sorts of go-betweens were required. These intermediary powers were conceived as personalities and identified with the angels in Scripture; chief among them was the Reason (*Logos*) of Greek philosophers. It was the Logos who spoke to Moses in the burning bush, and who is represented in the Hebrew Bible under the figure of the high priest. The approach to the Deity, unknowable, unnamable, yet supremely real, was effected by means of faith, an act of the will. For Philo, piety meant an ecstatic immersion in the Deity, a divine intoxication carrying the felt Presence of God to the soul.

Characteristics of Gnostic Teaching

Although many of the 'raw materials' of Gnosticism, drawn from Platonism, Zoroastrianism, and Judaism, were present before Christianity, it was only with the rise of Christianity that they were blended into an organised body of teaching attached to particular groups of people. Most Gnostics thought of themselves as followers of Christ, albeit a Christ who was pure spirit. The chief characteristics are:-

1   A sense of 'this world' and 'our bodily existence' as evil and the

cause of defilement to the soul. Because God is good and the material world is evil, he cannot have created it. The created order is therefore the work of lower, imperfect powers. In the earliest Christian systems these are angels, but later we find a Demiurge (Craftsman) often equated with the god of the Hebrew Bible, i.e. with the Jewish God and giver of the Law.

2   God is depth and silence, the unknowable, the absolute. He is believed to be the source of a spiritual hierarchy of beings called archons, who together form the pleroma, or realm of light. Knowledge of these archons enables the gnostic to recognise and return to his or her spiritual origin. The created order reflects nothing at all of the divine glory. Yet, people in their true nature are essentially akin to the divine, sparks of heavenly light trapped in physical bodies.

3   Salvation is the escape of the soul from the body to the heavenly realms above. However, those 'spiritual' individuals destined for salvation were ignorant of their heavenly origin. God therefore sent down to them a divine redeemer to bring salvation in the form of secret knowledge (gnosis) of their true nature and destiny. Thus awakened, the 'spirituals' escape from their prison-houses at death, and pass safely through the planetary spheres which are controlled by evil spirits, to be reunited with God in the realm of light.

The Gnostic estimate of the natural order as wholly alien from God led in some cases to manifestations of antinomianism, and in others to a very rigorous asceticism and rejection of this world. Carpocrates, for example, urged his disciples to sin; and his son Epiphanes taught that licentiousness was God's law.

Gnostic Leaders

The expansion of Gnostic speculation in the second century is directly linked to the names of particular teachers. Although there were a bewildering variety of forms, the features outlined above are common to the movement as a whole. The more important teachers were Valentinus and Marcion.

Valentinus

Valentinus studied philosophy at Alexandria. His disciples claimed that he had been educated by Theodas, a pupil of St. Paul, and was baptised a Christian. He lived at Rome from c.136 to c.165 where he aspired to be Bishop "on account of his intellectual force and eloquence" (*quia et ingenio poterat et eloquio*; see Tertullian *Adversus Valentinianos*, iv). He left the Christian community when he was passed over for that office c.140. On abandoning Rome for Cyprus c.160, Valentinus continued to develop his system of mythically derived religious philosophy. In broad outline, this postulates a supreme First Father or eternal Aeon, and by his side Sige (Silence) who is his Ennoia (Thought). From these emanate a succession of thirty aeons which together make up the *pleroma* or spiritual world. The youngest of these aeons, Sophia (Wisdom), gives way to lust and bears the Demiurge. The Demiurge creates the material part of man, but Sophia inbreathes her spiritual life into him unknown to the Demiurge, hence his 'spark of the divine'. Redemption is effected by the aeon Christ, the perfect expression of the spiritual world, who unites himself with the man Jesus (either at his conception or at his baptism) to bring humankind the saving *gnosis*.

Valentinus revered Paul as the primary source of the Gnostic tenet of 'secret' wisdom: 'The wisdom I proclaim is God's secret wisdom, which is hidden from mankind, but which he had already chosen for our glory even before the world was made,' (*1 Cor* 2.7.). In some Valentinian systems the Pauline categories of flesh, soul, and spirit were used to define the three classes of human beings, of whom the 'spirituals' alone (i.e. the Gnostics) were assured of salvation.

Valentinus was probably the most influential of the Gnostics. He had a large following and several of his disciples founded schools of their own. They included, in the east, Theodotus, and in the west, Ptolemy and Heracleon. Heracleon's highly allegorising commentary on St. John's Gospel is the earliest known commentary on a New Testament book.

St. Irenaeus, Tertullian and St. Clement of Alexandria all wrote against Valentinus' teachings.

Marcion

Marcion was born at Sinope on the shore of the Black Sea, the son of a Bishop. He came to Rome some time after 138 CE where he fell under the influence of Cerdo, a Gnostic Christian, who convinced him that the God of the Old Testament was to be distinguished from the God of the New Testament: the one embodying justice, the other goodness. For accepting, developing, and propagating these ideas, Marcion was excommunicated for heresy in CE 144, but the movement he headed became both widespread and powerful.

The basis of Marcion's theology is a sharp religious dualism. He contrasts a vain and angry creator with a transcendent god who bears no intrinsic relation to the created world at all. The creator god demands and ruthlessly exacts strict justice; he creates the material world of which man, body *and* soul, is part – a radical departure from the usual Gnostic tenet that it is only man's body which is part of the physical order. The other god, the kind god, out of sheer goodness takes pity on humankind and sends his son Jesus Christ to rescue it.

According to Marcion, this contrast of law and grace was fully understood by St. Paul alone. A much quoted text is Paul's Letter to the *Galatians* 3:13, 'Christ redeemed us'. The disciples of the creator had been inspired by him to crucify Christ, but their action only brought about the defeat of their god, for the kind god then demanded satisfaction from the creator who acknowledged that he had sinned in killing Jesus in ignorance; he would pay for his error by relinquishing his hold on the souls of all who should believe in him. For Marcion, then, men and women are saved through faith in the effect of Christ's act. In this he stands quite apart from the main stream of Gnosticism with its claim to a special revelatory *gnosis*. In this one respect, too, says Professor Chadwick, 'he was the most radical and to the church the most formidable of heretics,' (Henry Chadwick *The Early Church*, p39).

Marcion's dualism led him to reject the Hebrew scriptures outright. St. Paul, who so clearly understood the contrast of law and grace, was his hero, and he regarded all Christian writings that seemed to harmonise Jewish biblical traditions with Christian ones as suspect. The only Scriptures he accepted were ten of the Pauline Epistles (he either rejected or did not know the Epistles to Timothy and Titus) and the Gospel According to Luke (after he had expurgated it of Judaising elements). He rejected all allegorical methods of interpretation.

Marcion's many opponents included Bishop Dionysius of Corinth, St. Irenaeus, St. Theophilus and St. Hippolytus.

Relations with Christianity

Gnosticism nearly swallowed up Christianity in its attempt to identify the Christian Faith with the mystical thought of the Hellenistic world. The attractiveness of the Gnostic systems was that they offered disciples release from the dominance of the material world by contemplation of the rational or spiritual order. The weakness of Gnostic thought was that it left the whole material basis of man's life (including, e.g. his sexual life, work, and the economic order) unredeemed and unredeemable.

The use of Paul's thought by the Gnostics was to some extent countered by the composition of *1 and 2 Timothy* and *Titus* by a Pauline school (e.g. *1 Timothy* 6:20, 'Timothy, keep safe what has been entrusted to your care. Avoid the profane talk and foolish arguments of what some people wrongly call "Knowledge."').

As Christian teachers sought to refute the heresy they insisted on those very points that their Gnostic opponents had called into question:-

1   There is only one God, and he is the creator of all that is. Gnosticism's Demiurge ridicules the work of God in creation and removes him far beyond the galaxies. But the Christian God is not isolated from the material world.

2   The material creation is originally and fundamentally 'good', not evil. It was after God had finished creating the physical universe that evil was introduced.

3   Matter and spirit are not antagonistic but complementary.

4   The human body, as well as the human soul, is the subject of Christ's redemption, and in consequence shares the same resurrection: '. . .we ourselves, who have the first fruits of the Spirit, groan inwardly as we wait for adoption as sons, the redemption of our bodies,' (*Romans* 8:23). Gnostics saw resurrection as the recovery of the divine spark in man from the ashes of its material prison.

5   At the resurrection the entire physical universe will be perfected and glorified (i.e. restored to its original state), and become a suitable environment for redeemed humanity. Gnostic devaluation of the material world implied that nothing from it would play a role in salvation.

6   Jesus is God become man. The Church Fathers pointed out that Gnosticism's denial of the reality of the body of Jesus and consequently of his genuine manhood meant that he was completely different from the rest of the human race, i.e. he could not suffer as we do. Indeed, some Gnostic writings even speak of the Saviour looking on with laughter as the evil powers thought they were killing him. Such a view makes the life of

Jesus 'nothing more than one of the old Greek myths about the doings of the gods' (Alan Richardson).

Influence

The development of Christian doctrine was to a large extent a reaction against Gnosticism. Christian leaders emphasised the rule of faith (the summary of the apostolic teaching) as a guide to interpreting Scripture and sharpened the confessions to declare the truths of the Gospel in such a way as to deny Gnostic tenets. They also moved to form the canon of the New Testament Scriptures, i.e. those books where the authentic apostolic tradition was to be found. On the institutional level, the Fathers strengthened the position of the local Bishop as the focus of unity through the doctrine of Apostolic Succession. Scholars believe that the Church survived, in part, because its strong organisational ties gave it a stability which the loosely organised and diverse Gnostic groups simply did not possess.

CHAPTER SIX

CONSTANTINE AND CHRISTIANITY

In the third century the Roman Empire extended from the north of Britain, along the Rhine and Danube to the Black Sea, and from Spain, across the territories of North Africa bordering the Mediterranean, to the Middle East and Asia Minor, south of the Black Sea.

The capacity of the state to control and administer this vast area was stretched to breaking point. In North Africa disturbances and riots, brigands and thieves created spasmodic troubles. On the northern frontiers there were serious and threatening waves of invasion from barbarian tribes. Stability and defence were uncertain and the costs of increased taxation to pay for the armies were widely unpopular.

The emperor Diocletian (234-305), an effective soldier and administrator, attempted to secure the future through two main policies – the organisation of an orderly succession of rulers and the restoration of the old religion centred on the emperor as the agent of Jupiter. The career of Constantine overturned both policies.

Diocletian's arrangements for the state were based upon the division of the empire into eastern and western sectors, with precedence given to the chief ruler of the eastern part (which was at that time the most threatened by invasion). Retirements and promotions were to be planned and orderly, and he gave a lead by resigning voluntarily in 305. His scheme failed. There was intermittent war as rival generals eliminated one another. In the west Constantine eventually became supreme ruler by capturing Rome in 312 (though his base was Trier in Germany). Licinius, based at Nicomedia, became ruler of the east but was defeated by Constantine in 324. Until his death in 337 Constantine was the supreme and undisputed ruler of the Roman Empire.

Diocletian and many of the ruling familes attributed the problems of the empire to the collapse of the old forms and standards of religion. Those who followed Christianity were deserting the religion of their ancestors and so undermining the state. Among pagan intellectuals who thought like this was Porphyry, a pupil of Plotinus. In about

300, he produced a substantial work *Against the Christians*. In this he argued that Christians were barbarians and their beliefs incompatible with civilisation. As apostates from the ancestral religion they deserved punishment. Such an attack, carefully and skilfully argued, suggests that Christian beliefs were gaining ground among all levels of society and it is believed that some of Diocletian's own household had adopted Christianity.

Diocletian embarked on a systematic persecution of the Church arguing that the state would suffer harm from failure to render to the gods due worship and sacrifice. Four edicts in 303-4 aimed at the suppression of Christianity. In the first, church property was to be confiscated and assemblies for worship forbidden. Two further edicts announced severe penalties for clergy who refused to sacrifice to the gods or who did not hand over copies of scripture to be burned. The fourth edict required the laity to offer sacrifice to the gods. Penalties involved fines, imprisonment, torture and death but the strictness of officials in imposing these penalties varied. The harshest persecution was experienced in North Africa, in Carthage, Numidia and Egypt.

The clergy were those most affected by the first three edicts and they met official demands in different ways. In some areas it was not thought a very serious matter to hand over church plate, liturgical books or scriptures. Sometimes heretical writings were substituted and some of the plate was hidden. Everywhere it was considered that sacrifice to pagan gods was apostasy. Many clergy and laity would not compromise and suffered imprisonment, torture and martyrdom. But overall it was found that persecution was more disruptive to civil order than allowing Christians to worship.

Persecution ended officially with the Edict of Milan in 313, issued jointly by Constantine and Licinius (Stevenson, 1957, p300). Permission was granted 'to the Christians and to all others the full authority to follow whatever worship each man has desired.' Toleration was justified as follows: 'whereby whatsoever divinity dwells in heaven may be benevolent and propititious to us and to all who are placed under our authority.' The edict offers toleration for all forms of religious worship and provides for the return of property confiscated from the Church. Compensation is to be given from the imperial treasury.

These provisions recognise that the policy of persecution to root out Christianity had failed to produce the social peace and harmony both rulers most desired at that time.

Constantine's conversion

Constantine is known as the first Christian emperor; but, in spite of ample documentation, the circumstances of his conversion and the nature of his Christian beliefs have been the subject of extensive and, in the end, indecisive speculation. None of the contemporary sources can be taken at face value partly because their style is full of the courtly exaggerated imagery required at the time and partly because the writers have aims other than producing a reliable and objective historical account.

Constantine's family background was sympathetic to Christianity and his father, who ruled a substantial part of the western empire, did not enforce Diocletian's edicts of persecution. Initially Constantine showed allegiance to the sun-god Apollo. From 310, his coins bore the image of Apollo, the unconquerable sun (*sol invictus*), closely resembling his own profile placed adjacent to it. It is reported by a pagan writer of 310 that he made gifts to the most famous shrine to Apollo in Gaul and experienced a vision of the god in which he was promised victory and a reign of thirty years. Apollo appeared on his coins until 319.

Constantine's most significant campaign was in 312 when he invaded Italy. He went on to attack and capture Rome after the Battle of Milvian Bridge. This success was preceded by an experience which led Constantine to adopt a Christian symbol for his banners. The two chief accounts of this episode do not agree on the details. Lactantius' account was written before 318 and, as he became tutor to Constantine's son, he had access to those who had been with Constantine on his campaigns. He writes of a vision in which Constantine was directed to place a cross on the soldiers' shields (Stevenson, 1957, p298). Eusebius of Caesarea (see below) wrote a *Life of Constantine* in 338 as an obituary. This reports Constantine's statement on oath that he had a vision in which he saw a cross with the inscription *In hoc signe vinces* (Conquer by this sign). That night he had a dream in which he was told to use this sign 'as a safeguard in all engagements with his enemies.' This sign was developed into a characteristic symbol known as the *labarum*, a cross with an upright curved over, combining the Greek letters chi, rho, the first two letters of 'Christ' (Stevenson, 1957, p299).

Eusebius' account is part of an extended narrative of Constantine's whole reign and achievements as a Christian emperor, or rather as an ideal Christian emperor. It has been called 'a triumph of circumlocution and reticence' (Drake, 1976, *In praise of Constantine*, p8) In earlier times it was taken to be an objective historical account and has coloured many subsequent versions of Constantine's reign. There was no deliberate distortion but Eusebius' intention to be 'a kind of interpreter' warns us to be careful.

Most scholars accept that Constantine had become Christian by 312. He believed he was entrusted with a divine mission to convert the Roman Empire to Christianity and that God's wrath would descend upon him if he did not fulfil this. However, for reasons of state his personal beliefs could not immediately over-ride all other considerations. In Rome pagan worship and ceremonies were stronger than elsewhere and it was common sense and caution which stopped Constantine from a direct challenge to paganism.

He was however in a curious position. He was not baptised until 337 when he knew he was dying. He had Christian advisers in his entourage but it is not at all clear what understanding he had of Christian faith and, as a soldier, he was not of a speculative turn of mind. As a ruler he acted so as to make his subjects understand his religious preference, providing large and expensive church buildings, lavish gifts and privileges for the clergy. One other point is evident over a period of time: his edicts and speeches show a gradual decrease in the importance and power allowed to pagans.

In the earlier part of his reign Constantine's chief Christian adviser was Ossius, Bishop of Cordova. He was well educated and came from a wealthy family. He had a strong attachment to orderliness in church organisation, a trait which probably appealed to Constantine and influenced him in some of his policies.

Constantine: Emperor of the West

When he became ruler of the west, Constantine made magnificent gifts to the church. In Rome the land and endowment of the Lateran church came from a former palace and a shrine was built for St Peter's tomb. These and many other churches in Italy and the western provinces were provided with expensive building materials, rich decoration and ornament, valuable gold, silver and jewelled treasure and fine new copies of scripture. The bishops of Rome and numerous other bishops were provided with revenues, partly to allow their clergy to fulfil their vocation without the need to earn their living and partly for charitable purposes. In this way ample money, clothing and shelter were provided for the poorest in society.

Several items of legislation were designed to improve the status of the clergy. Property confiscated during the persecutions was to be restored. The church could also receive bequests, as it had always done, but now at the express wish of a dying person, an innovation which put ties to religion above ties of family. Exemption was granted to the clergy from the considerable financial burden of civic duties.

It was made possible for slaves to be freed by their masters in public before a bishop, who provided the certificate of proof, formerly given by civil magistrates. But from 316 (and possibly before) it was assumed that in such a case the freed slaves would also be granted Roman citizenship. Slaves owned by clergy could also be freed by the verbal statement of their master on his deathbed.

Constantine avoided any outright challenge to pagan beliefs and customs, but he made a number of changes which moved society in a Christian direction. In 321 Sunday was declared to be a day for 'pleasant and fitting' activities (Stevenson, 1957, p333). No legal work was permitted, except for the freeing of slaves. Agricultural labour was allowed but not the usual business and commerce, so the streets in towns became quieter. Christians were able to meet publicly for worship and soldiers were to recite a prayer specially composed for them by Constantine.

> We know you are God alone; we recognise in you our king. We call on you for aid. From you we receive victory, through you we are made greater than our enemies. We recognise your grace in present blessings and hope in you for the future. We all beseech you, we implore you to preserve our king, Constantine and his pious sons safe and victorious to the end of our days. (see MacMullen, 1970, p164)

There was clearly an ambiguity involved in this law. Constantine announced it as celebrating the Day of the Sun (Apollo) and this would have been widely understood and accepted by pagans. Christians were already marking it as the Lord's day and the regulations Constantine imposed suited Christian ideas. It proved to be a measure which, at the time, included everyone and was therefore unifying, and which has subsequently remained a feature of the western world.

Among other items of legislation Constantine allowed lawsuits to be transferred at any stage from civil courts to the arbitration of a bishop, against whose judgment there was no appeal. This regulation may have referred to instances where both parties were Christian, but this is not certain. In any case, bishops were now being given powers formerly reserved for magistrates.

Crucifixion was eventually banned as a punishment but gladiatorial contests were still allowed, and to be sent to be a gladiator remained a mode of punishment. Branding on the face was banned as defiling the image of God. It was forbidden to expose children when their parents were unable to afford to bring them up and Constantine gave money to provide for them.

Constantine also tightened up the supervision of his officials and there was severe punishment for those found guilty of extortion, corruption or neglect. Justice was to be speedy and in general the weak and oppressed were protected.

Donatist Schism

Undoing the effects of his predecessors' persecutions was more complicated than Constantine could have foreseen. His intention was to restore property, to compensate for loss and to give the clergy privileges. The difficulty was that the church in North Africa was seriously divided, with rival claimants to the bishopric of Carthage. Who should benefit from Constantine's generosity?

Between 313 when the trouble began and 321 when Constantine gave up the contest, the Donatist conflict illustrates the changed relationship between church and state and the effects of this within the church itself.

Diocletian's persecution had been severe in Carthage and the adjacent Numidia. Attitudes taken towards those alleged to have given way and who then wanted to be received back into the church were sometimes quite harsh. There was a fanatical streak among the Numidian Christians. In addition to the required acts of penance and a period of waiting before being received back into communion, some insisted on re-baptism, re-ordination of clergy and re-consecration of bishops. In the period 306-312 (i.e. before the Edict of Milan) there was deep division and anger, accusation and counter-accusation.

In 313, Constantine sent a letter to Anulinus, Proconsul of Africa, requiring him to restore 'those things that belonged to the Catholic church of the Christians in any city,' whether they are now in the 'possession either of citizens or of any other.' This was followed up by a letter to Bishop Caecilian of Carthage, in 313, making available to him a sum of money for 'expenses to certain specified ministers of the lawful and most holy Catholic religion.' A further letter to Anulinus directs that clergy should be exempt from the duties of public office in order to concentrate upon their religious duties. 'For when they render supreme service to the Deity, it seems that they confer incalculable benefit on the affairs of state' (Stevenson, 1957, p302-4).

The wording of these letters suggests that Constantine was aware of divisions and probably took the advice of Bishop Ossius in writing to Bishop Caecilian, for there was a rival bishop, Donatus, whose supporters disputed the validity of Caecilian's ordination. Donatus came from the agricultural district of Numidia and claimed that Numidian bishops had not been present at the election of Caecilian and that his consecration was not acceptable since it had been carried out by one who had compromised during the persecution by handing over scriptures to the Roman officials. Along with the argument based on religious discipline there was also deep-rooted hostility to anything Roman in Numidia, whereas the urban population of Carthage was more cooperative with imperial governments.

The Donatists created serious disturbances, because Constantine's privileges and gifts to Caecilian's clergy were too valuable to be lost. Constantine was both perplexed and irritated that toleration of the Christian religion did not produce the unity and harmony he wanted. He was also concerned about the scandal and disgrace which delighted the pagan opposition. Donatists were sufficiently numerous for him to be anxious to satisfy them without harsh measures of repression and when they appealed to him to appoint bishops from Gaul to arbitrate he agreed, though in a modified form. He made Miltiades, Bishop of Rome, chairman of a panel of bishops – eleven from Italy, in addition to those from Gaul. None of the evidence brought against Bishop Caecilian was substantiated and Donatus himself was declared to have acted wrongly in the re-baptism and re-consecration of those who had lapsed.

Donatus refused to accept this judgment against him and the disturbances and agitation increased, so Constantine proposed to settle their 'mad fury' in a larger Council of bishops at Arles in 314.

He provided free transport and the expenses of lodgings for thirty three bishops with their servants. The decisions of the previous council were confirmed and a number of other points of church discipline were settled (Stevenson, 1957, p318-320; 321-325).

Constantine's handling of the affair is important because he became involved as emperor in deciding a matter internal to church discipline and he chose to do so by summoning a council of bishops. This close relationship between church and state set precedents for later history.

The Donatists were not in any way repressed by the verdicts against them. They continued to appeal; they produced forged documents as evidence; they occupied their rivals' churches. In Cirta they took by force the basilica Constantine had provided and he let them keep it, building a second basilica for the Catholics. By 321 Constantine had many other matters to occupy him, but it was already clear that harmony within the church was elusive and he did not want to persecute Christian groups.

Constantine: Emperor of the East

In spite of his acceptance of the Edict of Milan, which promised religious toleration, Licinius did not maintain this policy after about 320. Persecution of Christians began again and, in addition, Licinius imposed heavy taxation to pay for his armies and he became increasingly unpopular. He was defeated by Constantine at the Battle of Chrysopolis in 324.

As the undisputed ruler of the eastern empire, Constantine now began to fulfil his promises of improved government, lower taxation and religious toleration. His immediate objective was peace and order, so he did not attempt any form of suppression likely to lead to rebellion or public disorder. Though paganism had been discredited by the defeat of Licinius, pagans were allowed to keep their buildings but they were forbidden to make sacrifices. They were permitted to hold their private beliefs but could not make the customary public expression of them. They were not to attack Christians in any way and copies of Porphyry's influential work *Against the Christians* were to be destroyed.

Although Constantine did not go to any great lengths to enforce his edicts against sacrifice it became clear that henceforward Christians would receive preferential treatment. The property of Christians which had fallen into pagan hands during the persecutions was to be handed back and there was to be no compensation (in contrast to the earlier restitutions in the west). Those who had been exiled or put to forced labour in factories and mines were brought back and their positions restored to them. Appointments were offered to Christians in preference to pagans. Large sums of money were made available for the repair of damaged churches and the construction of new ones.

The capital of the east was Nicomedia but for Constantine this was too closely associated with Diocletian and pagan worship to be satisfactory for his own base. He determined to found a new city, as many ancient rulers had done before him, and his choice of site was partly guided by the strategic need to be near to the main threat to his borders from the Goths and Persians, and also close to the main economic strength of his empire. Constantinople, dedicated in 325, was to be a new Rome but free from any taint of paganism. It was provided with splendid churches and the decoration of its public buildings and squares used Christian rather than pagan motifs. Its citizens were granted a status equal to that of Roman citizens and in the course of time it became the centre of religion in the east as Rome was in the west.

Arian controversy

It was in 324, at the time when Constantine most wanted to stress the benefits of Christianity as the official religion, that serious controversy in the church became a public scandal with riots and civil disturbance erupting in a number of major cities in Egypt, Palestine, Syria and Asia Minor. It is not easy for us to comprehend how a matter of theological definition could arouse such antagonism. There were two contributory factors. In these areas of the Middle East there were numerous cities living in a state of tension and rivalry with one another and treasuring points of difference with pride. The general level of education was also relatively high. People were theologically well-informed and practised in the skills of analytic argument. One of the surprising features is the immoderate and often vicious language used in debate and the apparent lack of scruple in employing intrigue, slander and invective against opponents.

Arius was a priest in Baucalis, subject to Bishop Alexander of
Alexandria. Reports of his teaching have come to us chiefly from
sources hostile to his position and, since his views were declared to
be mistaken, he has usually been presented as peddling a dangerous
heresy. Recently a more sympathetic view is taken as it is realised
that, although his doctrine is understood to be unacceptable, his
intentions were sincere. A wider comprehension of the thinking of
his contemporaries has shown that he was attempting to find a way
of presenting the divine-human status of Jesus Christ in terms which
would satisfy Christian converts from pagan philosophies who still
operated within those concepts of divinity.

The most advanced philosophies of the early fourth century
understood divinity as absolutely incommunicable in its
transcendence. Many Christian attempts to explain the relationship
of Jesus Christ to the Godhead struck some thinkers as taking people
back to a form of polytheism. Their understanding of the complete
otherness of the divine also presented them with difficulties over the
creation of a material universe which clearly has the defects of
suffering and evil.

Arius' solution attempted to meet these difficulties by his conception
of Christ as having an intermediate status between God and man. He
was the instrument of God for the creation of the world and as such
he himself had first to come into being (hence the catch-phrase 'there
was when he was not'). Only the Father was eternal. But Jesus Christ
was clearly more than human and so was regarded as having the
special relationship of Son to Father. Unfortunately, Arius' concern
for logic led him to treat analogy and metaphor as literal definition.
However he could point to controversial passages of scripture which
appeared to support his position. (Key texts for Arius were *Proverbs*
8:22-25; *Colossians* 1:15; *John* 14:28)

Looking back, it is possible to recognise that just as Arius was
attempting to supply a pastoral need among some of his
contemporaries his opponents were also moved by pastoral concern.
They saw that a Christ who is neither fully God nor properly human
could never bring about salvation. The New Testament implies that
he was both divine and human, though how this could be so remains
a mystery. In the west, statements of belief were satisfied to affirm
what Christ is to believers: it was typical of the east to speculate on
what he is in himself.

The Council of Nicaea

Constantine saw the Arian controversy as debate between philosophers. He wrote to Alexander and Arius in 324 stating his desire for unity and peace (Stevenson, 1957, p352). He says they should not have got into a dispute in the first place and that their argument arose from 'the contentious spirit which is fostered by misused leisure.' If they enjoy argument as an intellectual exercise they should have kept the matter private, because others are confused and take sides because they do not grasp the intricacies of the problem. The issues discussed do not refer to central doctrine but to 'insignificant questions.'

Constantine's primary concern was to maintain peace among the estimated 60-80 million people he ruled, but his letter had little effect. The next proposal was to call a council of bishops in Ancyra (in Bithynia, Asia Minor) but before this could happen the church in Antioch, Syria fell into disarray. About fifty bishops had gathered there to settle the election of a new bishop and they chose Eustathius, an opponent of Arius. They went further and composed a statement of belief, intending it to be a test of orthodoxy. Eusebius, bishop of Caesarea (see above) was one of three who refused to accept it. He had been educated by teachers who held views similar to those of Arius' teachers, all of them influenced by Origen of Alexandria, but he did not take a rigid Arian position. All three were excommunicated, conditional upon confirmation at the planned council in Ancyra – which in fact took place at Nicaea in 325.

Constantine changed the location of the council to a town nearer to his capital, possibly because of threatened political unrest. It was about this time that Licinius (the former ruler of the east) was killed, though how far Constantine was implicated is unclear (Barnes, 1981, p214). It is possible that he did not grasp the theological issues involved in the controversy, but he certainly recognised the potential danger of the serious unrest in the major centres of population in the eastern part of his empire.

He claimed afterwards that the idea of a general council was his own. He summoned bishops from the west as well as from the east and provided free transport and lodging expenses (Stevenson, 1957, p358). Nearly three hundred came. Some were survivors who bore the scars of persecution. Some came from isolated districts and were probably not so much concerned about the issues to be debated as they were about promoting harmony in the church. Others were skilled in philosophical debate and others were primarily interested in administration and the promotion of their careers. The majority came from the east and the bishop of Rome, pleading age and infirmity, was represented by two presbyters.

There is no detailed record of the deliberations of the Council of Nicaea which continued for two months. A later historian named Socrates (380-450) said of it 'The situation was exactly like a battle fought by night for both parties seemed to be in the dark about the grounds on which they were hurling abuse at each other' (quoted by Frend, 1984, p498). Eusebius of Caesarea wrote a version of what took place in the form of a letter to his own church, but it must be remembered that he was most concerned about having the verdict of the Council of Antioch rescinded (Stevenson, 1957, p364).

Eusebius defended his position by offering the creed of his church as his statement of belief. Constantine (though he was not baptised) intervened in the debate to say he found nothing amiss in this formulation but he asked Eusebius to accept the addition of one word – *homoousios* (of the same substance). It is believed that Constantine's advisers prompted him to ask for this (Barnes, 1981, p215,379). With reluctance Eusebius agreed and it seems that Constantine's intervention made a full and open discussion impossible. A number of bishops produced a draft creed and after some argument over the exact meaning of certain phrases, all but two bishops from Libya signed it. Anathemas were pronounced on the main Arian statements (eg 'there was when he was not'). Arius and those who still supported him were exiled and the main Arian writings destroyed.

Two further points need to be made about the creed agreed at Nicaea. It was not, as some scholars have argued, a modified version of the statement put forward by Eusebius (see Kelly, 1972, p205-262). Nor is it what is popularly known as 'the Nicene Creed'. That formulation was agreed at Chalcedon 451, on the basis of the creed agreed at Constantinope 381. The link with Nicaea stems from a sixth century tradition which is now discredited but, to acknowledge this, the full title of 'the Nicene Creed' is the Niceno-Constantinopolitan Creed.

Having settled the Arian question for the time being, the Council of Nicaea moved on to other business. It established numerous canons of discipline (Stevenson, 1957, p358-364). Several referred to bishops. The special status of the bishops of Alexandria, Rome and Antioch was confirmed. The election of a new bishop was to be agreed by all the bishops of the province, in person if possible, or if not, in writing and certainly by no fewer than three meeting together and carrying out consecration. The chief bishop in each province should be informed of all that happens in its churches. Bishops would not be permitted to move from see to see – a rule directed against those who tried to follow a career structure.

The date of Easter was settled. A number of churches in the east had been accustomed to celebrating Easter at the time of the Jewish passover. Constantine was totally opposed to this because of the link with Judaism. The date followed by Egypt was agreed upon.

These decisions were communicated throughout the empire by letters from the bishops but Constantine also sent out letters, thus emphasising his role as a Christian emperor bringing peace to the Church. (For Constantine's view of Nicaea see Stevenson, 1957, p371).

The Council of Nicaea is important in the history of the Church as a turning point in its relations with the state, in its treatment of orthodoxy and in the development of the role of bishop.

The council met not primarily by the bishops' decision but in response to the emperor's summons. In this way its procedures resembled an imperial court of appeal and Constantine's presence and interventions had the effect of making its decisions look like imperial edicts.

The bishops in council were required to decide upon matters of orthodoxy although not all of them could be regarded as theologians fully aware of the issues. Nicaea was the first of a series of ecumenical councils used to formulate doctrine and define discipline. Constantine believed such a council had sufficient authority to require general acceptance of its decisions, but one result was that those who did not accept what the majority agreed were labelled heretics. In this way certain groups were excluded from the mainstream of Christianity perhaps too hastily. Constantine issued an edict about heresy, probably soon after the Council of Nicaea (though see Barnes, 1981, p224 for a different view). Those who did not conform were forbidden to hold meetings and their books and property were confiscated. Unfortunately, the Church forgot its own experience of persecution and went along with Constantine's policy of repression.

The decisions of the Council greatly enhanced the role and status of bishops. Even before Constantine, groups of bishops had maintained informal contact with one another, for mutual support and recognition and for consultation in time of crisis. This network was important also for ordinary church members, who relied on their bishops to give them certificates to establish their position if they moved to another district. This acceptance by other congregations was essential if help were needed, or support in times of illness or in old age, especially for those who had handed over their property to the church when they were converted.

What had been an informal pattern became established formally after Nicaea. Constantine channelled gifts of money through bishops for the relief of poverty and began to use them for functions formerly belonging to magistrates. Bishops therefore acquired considerable power and influence and became advisers to the emperor. Perhaps at times he treated them as imperial bureaucrats.

The Christian Empire

During the reign of Constantine the Church passed from a situation of threat and suffering to a position of favour and privilege. The change was sudden and the Christian leadership was unprepared for new responsibilities and had little chance to evaluate beforehand the implications of state approval and patronage.

Constantine believed he was the agent of God to bring concord to the empire, and though he could not receive the same honours as his predecessors who claimed to be divine, he could still be set apart for veneration. Now that the emperor was Christian, the Church could accept his rule and there was widespread desire for absolute monarchy as a safeguard against chaos and anarchy. There was therefore a readiness to work with Constantine and to believe that present prosperity was a vindication for the martyrs of persecution.

The positive discrimination Constantine gave the Church was also intended to win converts to make Christianity in reality the religion of the empire. There was to be no compulsion but there were clear benefits in becoming Christian. For some, to be Christian was recognised as the precondition for worldly success and many of the ruling families in the pagan empire made a smooth transition to become the ruling families of the Christian empire. Among them were those who genuinely believed that Christianity was a practical means of regenerating society, but their adherence did not involve an inward attachment. For many converts the clergy were unable to provide the necessary grounding in the faith even though Constantine saw to it that there were new buildings for worship and ample resources. Perhaps the meaning of the Christian faith was diluted and distorted through the sudden expansion of numbers but at the time there was little choice about receiving them.

Society as a whole benefitted gradually from Christian standards of morality and attitudes to work and family life. Many of the institutions remained but more humane considerations permeated them. Slavery was not abolished but criticism needs to be related to the prevailing situation. Slaves had a fixed place in society which depended upon their labour in agriculture and in certain industries. Constantine was not seeking disruption and the Church had no thought-out programme of social reform to offer him. Instead, the situation was accepted but greater attention was paid to the obligations of master and slave to one another, the duties of providing for slave families within a household and the honour and dignity of service. In the fourth century the Church did not see the recognition of human worth diminished by slave status.

State intervention in the affairs of the Church brought some immediate benefit, but, in the long term, led to difficulties which have persisted down the centuries. If Christianity was to unify the empire, Constantine believed it must itself be united. He did not impose his own opinions, but urged the Church to settle controversy by making clear decisions over matters of doctrine and discipline. This was to assume that one right answer could be found for every question, but experience has shown that Christian belief does not altogether fit that requirement. The attempt to bring unity, perhaps too soon in the Church's development, resulted in division and exclusion. State involvement also led Church leaders to turn to the government to enforce their decisions. Before long it became possible for strong rulers to look back to such precedents and claim the right to enforce their own religious policies.

The founding of Constantinople as the new capital tilted the balance of the empire towards its eastern provinces which had long been important centres of civilisation and commerce. Constantine's policies of state intervention in the affairs of the Church were to some extent determined and shaped by the problems of government in these regions. In the west the local churches looked to Rome for leadership. The overall level of culture and civilisation was simpler than in the east and the church correspondingly less troubled by internal theological division. These differences between the eastern and western regions of the empire help to account for the growing separation of their churches and distinctive lines of development.

CHAPTER SEVEN

THE GREAT SCHISM

The word *schism* implies separation with a clean break, in this case between the Christian Church of the eastern, Byzantine part of the Roman Empire (now known as the Orthodox Church) and the western Roman Catholic Church. But scholars have reached no agreement about the date or the cause of this rupture. They tend to describe the separation as a drifting apart and a disjointed and gradual process. The possible reasons are identified only with hindsight, and even so, no single theory appears to be totally satisfactory.

The differences which developed in doctrine and practice were debated at length and eventually became subordinate to the issue of authority in the church. Both east and west accepted the primacy of Rome, as the ancient capital of the empire and as one of the earliest Christian centres linked with the apostles Peter and Paul. Yet, as time went on, there was fundamental disagreement over the full implications of this term *primacy*. Bishops in the east often consulted the pope but they also frequently rejected his judgments. From time to time there was mutual excommunication and then, later on, reconciliation. The point of irrevocable rupture is often put at 1054, because all subsequent attempts at reunion failed, but at the time it was not recognised as schism.

Political background

For a thousand years after Constantine's founding of a Christian empire the problems facing the eastern and western regions drew them apart.

From the fifth century the western provinces were over-run by Germanic migrations: the Visigoths in southern France and Spain, the Vandals in North Africa, the Ostrogoths and Lombards in Italy. The Christian Church survived with difficulty. By the eighth century most of the newly established kingdoms had become Christian through the conversion of their rulers, but their customs and attitudes influenced their understanding and practice of Christianity making it different in a number of ways from developments in the east during the same period. As well as this many of the converts adopted Arian beliefs, especially the Visigoths in Spain and France, until at the Council of Toledo in 589, Arianism was formally rejected. In 753 the Lombards took Ravenna and the pope, having appealed unsuccessfully for help from the emperor in the east, sought alliance with the Franks. This began an association whereby the pope gained a measure of independence from the Byzantine east, both in the affairs of state as well as in ecclesiastical matters. In return, however, he was subject to political influence. Charlemagne, the forceful ruler of the Franks, was crowned Holy Roman Emperor in 800, and to enhance his prestige he built up the notion of Rome as a great ecclesiastical centre to counterbalance the absence of an established culture and civilisation comparable with that of the Byzantine empire.

In the meantime the eastern region lost territory in the first waves of Islamic expansion, during the seventh and eighth centuries. The more serious threat came in the eleventh century with the attacks of the Muslim Seljuk Turks. During the same period the Saracens and Normans attacked territory in the Mediterranean, some belonging to the east and some to the west. The common enemy temporarily drew both regions together in their need for mutual support.

In response to appeals for help, the western rulers, whose military strength was now superior to that of the east, organised a series of Crusades against Islam. Those involved began to be aware of differences in forms of Christianity. The Crusaders behaved with great arrogance towards eastern Christians, established their own churches and provided their own clergy. In 1204, during the Fourth Crusade, the western army captured and devastated Constantinople and actually set up its own government there for about 60 years.

Attacks from Islamic armies were renewed many times until at length Constantinople was captured by the Turks in 1453. Islam continued to be a threat well into the sixteenth century, affecting the policy of Charles V, the emperor at the time of the Reformation.

In the earlier part of this period, the bishop of Rome was compelled to take over many of the functions of a secular ruler, simply to maintain order in the chaos of invasion and the disruption of the state. Gregory the Great (590-604) was a notable example of such leadership. Similarly, with the collapse of Christian congregations in the west it was inevitable that Rome's importance as the Christian centre should be enhanced. Later, alliance with the Holy Roman Emperor gave the pope further encouragement to claim supreme authority in church affairs of every kind.

In the Byzantine empire there were several patriarchs of Christian churches in important cities claiming mutual recognition. They were closely associated with the emperors who followed Constantine's policy of trying to encourage unity among a heterogeneous population by the unifying influence of Christianity. In the centuries after his death, the wealth and strength of the eastern empire led to a disregard for the loss to the barbarians of the barely civilised western provinces. When at length help was needed in the contest against Islam, the two parts of the former Roman Empire, and also their churches, had become strangers to one another.

Authority within the church

Constantine and his successors believed that strong government required harmony within the Church. Disputes should be settled firmly and rapidly by representative councils of bishops. General or ecumenical councils were called by the emperors, financed by them and, of the seven recognised by both Catholic and Orthodox Churches, six were held in or near Constantinople and the seventh not far away at Ephesus. To be counted as ecumenical, representation from the main Christian centres was expected, with the assumption that the council's decisions would then be regarded as authoritative for the whole Church. Among these centres were Jerusalem, Antioch, Alexandria, Constantinople and Rome.

The subjects discussed were matters of doctrine or discipline and clearly stated decisions were required by the government so that administrators would know how to judge controversial situations in their provinces. For example, in the eastern region there was frequent argument over the orthodoxy of rival candidates for a bishopric, though accusations of heresy could have masked quite different causes of dispute. Unfortunately the political pressure to define points of doctrine sometimes led to premature decisions and an unnecessary exclusion of alternative viewpoints. As a result there was a proliferation of groups labelled heretical and often subject to unpleasant social consequences. It is sometimes claimed that the relatively rapid conversion of the Middle East to Islam can be traced to the uncharitable attitudes of the 'orthodox' believers who, as a result of council definitions, made the dividing lines too rigid.

The first expansion of Islam in the seventh and eighth centuries, effectively removed three of the patriarchies from exerting influence on developments in the Church. Jerusalem, Antioch and Alexandria were in regions conquered by the Arabs and, although Christian churches survived, they were isolated from one another and preoccupied with resisting widespread conversions to Islam among the general population. Consequently Constantinople became the most influential Christian centre of the Byzantine Empire and its importance was enhanced by its closeness to the emperor's court and its wealth.

But this development at the official level did not affect the relations between the clergy and laity in the east. The general level of culture and civilisation was high and there were numerous cities of moderate size. Greek was the language of the church, of academic study and of everyday life (apart from remote rural areas). Clergy often combined their liturgical duties with earning a living and were therefore in touch with all sections of society. Because of these conditions, discussion of religion was not restricted to a sub-section of the population – the educated clergy. Theological exploration and argument could be carried on intelligently by everyone. Sometimes the disputes in local churches resulted in riots and disturbances and the government's desire for effective machinery to settle conflicts is understandable. At the same time it is clear that edicts issued by clergy were not necessarily received meekly and obediently by the laity, who had their own opinions.

It is out of this general situation that appeals were sometimes made to Rome, as the major Christian church of the west. The bishops of the east naturally used polite expressions in framing their letters, calling the pope father and teacher, but whereas the pope may have taken such expressions literally, those who wrote in this way did not necessarily mean that they believed the pope's statements had to be received as final and authoritative judgments.

Another distinctive feature of the east was the contrast between extreme sensitivity to minor differences in theology, which were condemned, and a relaxed attitude to differences in custom and practice. The cosmopolitan character of the Byzantine empire dated from the fourth century BCE from Alexander's conquests, and the diversity of cultural features was accepted as normal.

Attitudes to authority in the west developed differently. After the collapse of the Roman Empire the western areas had to be re-evangelised and Rome was the chief source of such missions. Their success depended on the collaboration of the numerous rulers who established themselves after the great Germanic invasions. There were conversions of whole tribes who had a very limited understanding of the Christian faith and easily mingled it with pagan beliefs and practices. Consequently it became increasingly important to try to establish some kind of uniformity, and Rome naturally became the source of authority in ecclesiastical matters.

From the fourth century Latin became the liturgical language of the Church and, because of the variety of languages spoken throughout the west, Latin also became the language of the educated, almost synonymous as a group with the clergy. Therefore there grew up a separation between those capable of discussing theology and those who were required to receive instruction without additional intellectual grounding. A further consequence of the predominant use of Latin was that Greek became an unknown language in the Church. Neither the New Testament nor the major Greek Church Fathers were studied in the original. Therefore the authoritiative sources of theology were restricted and part of the ancient tradition neglected.

The increasing separation of attitudes and interests is reflected in the choice of popes. From 654-752 there were 17 popes, of whom 11 came from a Greek-speaking background. From 752-1054 there were 61 popes, of whom 60 came from a mainly Latin-speaking background (Southern, 1970, p65). Communication between east and west was severely limited by difference of language and along with this went different attitudes to a range of issues, including the role and source of authority.

Differences in doctrine and practice

The specific differences between the Catholic and Orthodox churches, which now seem so marked, grew up gradually and were often responses to local heretical tendencies. Their importance grew as they become bargaining issues in negotiations between the two sides.

The central problem of doctrine rests with a phrase added to the western Latin translation of the Niceno-Constantinopolitan Creed of 381 (known as the Nicene Creed, see previous chapter). The controversial words refer to the Holy Spirit 'who proceeds from the Father *and the Son*' (Latin: *filioque*). The precise origin of the addition is unknown but there is documentary evidence of its use at the Council of Toledo in Spain in 583, called to reject Arianism. The Latin version of the creed was recited and included *filioque*. It reinforced correct theology but no one believes that a deliberate insertion was made. At that time, the creed was not widely used in the west, and it could easily have been assumed that the Latin was an accurate translation of the original Greek.

This form of the creed was adopted by Charlemagne, whose advisers came from Spain, and used in his chapel at Aachen. His policy was to require uniformity in his domains and so the *filioque* clause was widely used. But the popes resisted formal acceptance of the words, partly to avoid irritating the eastern bishops. They could evade the issue because at that time the creed was not recited in the form of Mass used in Rome. The first occasion of its use there was probably not until 1014 when the Emperor Henry II insisted on the creed being included at his coronation.

In the meantime eastern theologians, practised in the analysis of error, objected to the phrase for two reasons. First, they considered it illegitimate for an addition to be made to a statement agreed by an ecumenical council unless by formal agreement at a subsequent council. For them the final authority in matters of doctrine was a council of bishops. Second, there were objections to the phrase itself.

Photius (820-891) was one such critic. He was primarily a scholar, who became patriarch of Constantinople. In response to the pope who queried his appointment he made his general position clear. 'Everyone must preserve what is defined by common ecumenical decisions, but a particular opinion of a Church Father or a definition issued by a local council can be followed by some and ignored by others '(quoted by Meyendorff, 1974, p101).

Theological objection to the *filioque* clause came from the particular eastern emphasis on the Father as the source and fountainhead of divinity. For Photius the words destroyed the monarchy of the Father. Further, the Christian experience was of the Spirit as a distinct person, as with the experience of the other two persons of the Trinity. As understood from an eastern theological perspective the *filioque* clause seemed liable to renew third and fourth century heresies which confused the persons of the Trinity. The Church Fathers whose writings supplied insight into the doctrine of the Spirit and of the Trinity wrote in Greek whereas in the west theologians relied on the Latin writings of Augustine. As Meyendorff points out, neither side really grasped the position of the other and they drew from different sources among the Church Fathers (see Meyendorff, 1974, p92; Kelly, 1972, p358).

During the ninth century Boris of Bulgaria was converted to Christianity and missionaries from both west and east hastened to instruct the general population, as both parts of the empire attempted to extend their influence in the area. The clergy of both sides now realised the extent of their different practices and customs (in addition to the wording of the creed and the underlying difference in theology). Whereas the Greek speaking clergy did not object to diversity in practices, the Latin speaking clergy found diversity unacceptable and required the Bulgarians to conform to western custom.

Clergy from the east were married and wore beards, which was meant to signify that the flesh was not evil. It was a deliberate challenge to earlier heresies which focused on the spiritual at the expense of the material. With a different background the western clergy followed the discipline of being clean-shaven and celibate.

Confirmation was conducted by a bishop in the west, but by a priest in the east. Practices during Lent also differed: priests from the west required fasting on Saturdays but ate milk, butter and cheese which were forbidden in the east. In the west *Alleluia* was used only at Easter and the eucharistic bread was unleavened. In the east leavened bread was the rule.

These differing practices developed during the period when each side was preoccupied with its own affairs and separated by language and circumstance. But on the mission field they caused many problems where new converts needed to be given consistent teaching and discipline. The outcome was the setting up of two kinds of churches – those who followed the Latin rite and those who followed the Greek. (During the Second World War the papal legate who had to cope with the consequences of this division was the man who became Pope John XXIII and the experience influenced his attitude towards ecumenism. See chapter nine on the Second Vatican Council.)

In spite of these differences and the antagonism they engendered the Church at the end of the ninth century still believed itself to be one. Arguments and controversy continued as each side justified its position until the events of 1054.

Norman attacks on Sicily and southern Italy brought the pope and the emperor together for mutual support. They agreed that the pope would provide military help to protect territory belonging to the emperor and, in return, the emperor would allow the pope to extend his jurisdiction in these areas. This would be at the expense of the patriarch of Constantinople who had ecclesiastical control of the territory at the time. This patriarch, Michael Cerularius, heard of the arrangement and, along with others, drew attention to the differences in practices between the Latin and Greek rite churches, and closed all the Latin rite churches in Constantinople that refused to modify their customs. The pope (in spite of being a captive of the Normans) wrote to assert his authority and sent legates to Constantinople to settle matters with the emperor and to call the patriarch to obedience. The patriarch refused to meet the pope's legates, was excommunicated by them and in turn excommunicated the legates.

At the time of the First Crusade, 1098, the pope endeavoured to restore relations, and it probably seemed that the separation was just one more incident in a long series of such conflicts. Unfortunately the years of the Crusades served to harden the differences and make them more pronounced.

At the Council of Lyons, 1274, the Byzantine Emperor (who had regained Constantinople from the Crusaders) hoped to negotiate reunion. The Greek delegates ceded all that was asked including the definition of the *filioque* clause as meaning 'the Holy Spirit eternally proceeds from the Father and the Son.' When they returned home the Byzantine clergy and laity refused to accept what had been agreed.

The situation of the Byzantine empire grew more desperate as the attacks of the Turks increased. In the hope of gaining military aid, a further attempt to restore relations was made at the Council of Ferrara-Florence in 1438-9. The pope was anxious to establish his authority at home since it was being challenged by those who wanted councils to be the final voice of authority. A statement was eventually agreed.

> 'We recognise the pope as sovereign pontiff, vicegerent and vicar of Christ, a shepherd of all Christians, ruler of the church of God; saving the privileges and rights of the patriarchs of the east.' (Quoted Latourette, 1954, p621)

The last phrase was left deliberately ambiguous and undefined.

When the eastern delegates returned home they found that the patriarchs repudiated the agreement and clergy and laity both totally rejected the compromise.

Any further chance of reconciliation was lost when Constantinople was occupied by the Turks in 1453 and by then the west was beginning to be caught up in the events of the Reformation.

It is sad that little seems to have been done to promote mutual understanding. The Greeks regarded those in the west as little better than barbarians and did not know of the great intellectual advances made in the eleventh and twelfth centuries. It was not until the fourteenth century that the Latin writings of Augustine and Aquinas (and other theologians) were translated into Greek. Similarly the west was ignorant of Greek theology until the fifteenth century when scholars began to learn Greek and acquired printed copies of the Greek Church Fathers. By then misunderstandings had become deeply rooted.

Political factors were involved at every stage. There was rivalry between the emperors of west and east and the church was used by each side to claim power and influence. Sometimes popes and emperors bargained military support for ecclesiastical benefits. None of the main actors emerge with credit. Yet alongside these events the Christian faith persisted and in recent years the west has shown interest in and appreciation of Orthodox spirituality. Since the Second Vatican Council the Orthodox Church and the Roman Catholic Church have entered into dialogue with one another once more.

CHAPTER EIGHT

THE REFORMATION

Some scholars find the word 'Reformation' an unsatisfactory description for the sixteenth century changes and divisions in the western church. They want to distinguish 'reforms' which were for the renewal of the Church from the fundamental changes in doctrine introduced by the Reformers. But this is not a simple distinction because the Reformers believed they were returning to the pure church of the earliest years.

The period of the Reformation (adopting the customary terminology) is well documented, for it coincided with the invention of movable type printing, and those involved made good use of the opportunity to publish their ideas. The events have also been worked over extensively by historians, both Catholic and Protestant, searching for plausible explanations of such major changes. The general conclusion seems to be that the Reformation is a many-sided . phenomenon, characterised by the interaction of several political social and intellectual factors and stirred by the impulse of Martin Luther's religious experience and thought. Hillerbrand (1975, p189) puts it a little differently. 'No single factor or party or person deserves eminent credit or blatant blame.'

In the sixteenth century, much of Europe was acquiring a sense of national identity with individual rulers claiming independence both from the authority of the Church and from the Holy Roman Emperor. The regions furthest away from Italy, though Christian, found Roman notions of law and hierarchy alien to their own traditions and Christianity seemed to be too closely allied to Mediterranean culture. Conversely, Rome was not well-informed or even much interested in distant developments or disaffection.

The flow of money to Rome was a constant source of annoyance. The medieval administration set up in the eleventh century, the Curia, had become both inefficient and corrupt. Popes combined secular and religious roles and as rulers had to finance the costs of government, of a court, of war and of building. They raised money as other rulers did, but also used the dubious methods of 'sale' of appointments and of fees for dispensations, privileges and other benefits. Secular rulers, also in need of money, objected to the treasure going out of their territory and countered by building shrines and centres of pilgrimage to encourage the flow of money inwards. They were also increasingly irritated that the clergy, often controlling the revenues of large states, were exempt from taxation. This privilege, granted by Constantine, had little justification more than a thousand years later.

It is hard to assess the extent of corruption, immorality and ignorance among the clergy. Protestant sources paint a grim picture and later Catholic reforms show the need of improvement in pastoral care. Yet, as Chadwick shows (1964, p22-24), there was growing popular devotion and an increased demand for spiritual books. It may be that criticisms arose at least partly from higher expectations rather than from a marked decline in the quality of religious provision.

Among intellectuals there was growing distaste for the methods of teaching in universities. All higher education was provided by the Church and great advances had been made in the early medieval period. Before the invention of printing, manuscripts were annotated in great detail with comments from the early Church Fathers. Paris, for example, was pre-eminent in the eleventh and twelfth centuries for a high standard of teaching, but, in time, lectures became endless commentary upon commentary, taking students further and further from the text.

In the late fifteenth century new possibilities arose. Latin was the normal language for academic study, but with the flight of scholars from regions overtaken by Turkish Islam, there was the chance to acquire a knowledge of Greek. Greek grammars were published in 1495, 1516 and 1518. Erasmus published a Greek New Testament in 1516. Reuchlin's Hebrew grammar became available in 1506 and Jacques Lefèvre d'Etaples published the Hebrew text of a number of Psalms in 1509. Printing also enabled scholars to establish collections of reference books and acquire copies of the early Church Fathers for detailed private study of the original text. The study of the bible in Hebrew and Greek inspired translations of scriptures into the vernacular so that the less highly educated could experience for themselves the revelation believed to be transmitted through scripture.

This intellectual and linguistic movement is known as humanism (though not with twentieth century connotations). It took many forms and though it often resulted in critical attitudes, it was not necessarily anti-religious. McGrath (1988, p32) characterises it as essentially the effort to return to classical models of literature, not so much for content as for style. Detailed textual examinations became an essential part of study and this exerted a profound influence on many Reformers. The most notable humanist author, Erasmus (1466-1536), in addition to his Greek editions of important works, wrote a number of books which attracted wide interest, partly for their elegance and wit and partly for their teasing but sharp criticism of aspects of church life. Nevertheless though he was attractive to many Reformers he did not join them and regretted the divisions they brought about.

Luther's religious development

Martin Luther (1483-1545) became an Augustinian monk at Erfurt, Saxony in 1501 and in 1511 he was appointed professor of biblical studies at the new University of Wittenberg. Between 1513 and 1519 he lectured on the Psalms, Romans, Galatians, Hebrews and again on the Psalms. Notes on these lectures remain and provide some evidence of his style of exegesis (i.e. the detailed explanation of the text) and of his treatment of doctrine. Caution must be used in drawing conclusions about the development of his thought during these years, because the notes come chiefly from his students and were later revised by Luther.

Luther's personal spiritual crisis took the form of a renewed relationship with God in reaction against what he believed to be the erroneous teaching he had previously received. Protestant and Catholic accounts of the matter differ. Protestants tend to use terms like new insight, breakthrough or a rediscovery of the original teaching of the Church. Catholics point to deficiencies in the training Luther received and also to the moderating features of the prayers he would have known and used, which, had he noticed them, could have preserved him from much distress and anguish. Luther's own account, written later in life, presents a vivid and forceful description in what many regard as exaggerated terms.

There is general agreement that Luther's theological understanding was shaped by the philosophy of the Franciscan William of Ockham (Occam) (1270-1349) though he learned it in a restricted form. The phrase 'Occam's razor' comes from the characteristic approach of this philosophy, known technically as Nominalism. Its guiding principle was to cut away the speculative systems of theology based on the reasoning methods of Aristotle and instead to start afresh from experience. This meant dispensing with the highly regarded theology of Aquinas. McGrath (1988, chapter 4) outlines the conclusion of recent research that there were two forms of Nominalism and that in the course of his development Luther moved from the first to the second.

In its theological application, the earlier form, known as *via moderna* took an optimistic view of human nature, believing it to be free and able to cooperate with the will of God. The relation between man and God was understood in terms of covenant, with each party having defined obligations. Provided an individual tried to fulfil what was required of him, God would respond. 'God will not deny his grace to whoever does what lies within him' (*facienti quod in se est Deus non denegat gratiam*). It is easily seen how this way of thinking could lead to the conclusion that people are saved by their own efforts, even to the extent of claiming that God would be obliged to reward them.

Luther's problem was that he did not believe himself capable of meeting the precondition of doing all that was required of him. In this he was influenced by the writings of Augustine which had become available in the eleven-volume edition of Amerbach in 1506. Many others of his generation were also influenced by the thought of Augustine (e.g. Calvin) so that the second form of Nominalism is known as *schola Augustiniana moderna*.

Augustine's emphasis was on the unmerited and undeserved grace of God which enabled human nature to overcome its weakness and its inability to meet divine demands. As he pondered the text of Romans, especially 1:17, Luther focussed on the concept of God's righteousness. In his day there was a tendency to stress the majesty and omnipotence of God and Luther understood God's righteousness from this perspective. Such a God exercised a justice which punished. But with growing conviction and clarity he came to a different understanding – that God, through grace, *gives* righteousness to the sinner who receives it in faith. There is therefore no precondition of merit for salvation.

Luther's stand against Rome

'When you look at St Peter's you are looking at one of the primary causes of the Reformation . . . because they needed money to build it

. . . They made money by selling indulgences' (Henry Chadwick, The Tablet, 6 April 1991).

The practice of indulgences arose in the early middle ages and what was intended by them was easily misunderstood. Anyone who repented and confessed his sins expected to be given a penalty to be undertaken now, and the accompanying absolution given by the priest signified forgiveness in the sight of God. The word indulgence, as in modern usage, suggests kindness, and sometimes a less exacting penalty was substituted for the normal one. No truly sincere Christian would claim a substitute but, as many were inadequately taught, it became the popular (mis)understanding that payments of money (for good works such as building a church or contributing to a Crusade) would cover all that was required, often with the neglect of inward contrition and repentance.

The scandal which dismayed Luther and which came to his notice through his pastoral duties, began in 1513 when Albrecht of Brandenburg aged 24 years wished to combine the offices of Archbishop of Magdeburg, administrator of Halberstadt and Archbishop of Mainz. To do this he had to pay large sums of money to the pope for each office separately, for permission to hold all three at once and for being underage for any of them. He borrowed the money from the Fugger banking family of Augsburg and the pope's advisers proposed to him that he should promote for eight years the preaching of indulgences for the building of St Peter's in Rome, half the proceeds to go to Rome and the other half to be for his own use to pay interest on his loan. Frederick, Elector of Saxony would not permit indulgences to be preached in his territory, not for religious scruple, but because he did not wish money to leave his lands for the benefit of Albrecht or the pope.

In 1517 Luther set out his objections in a letter to Albrecht, Archbishop of Mainz and then sent his famous Ninety-Five Theses to all bishops in the area. It was only when he had no satisfactory replies that he gave them to scholars in Wittenberg. (The story of his nailing them to the door of Wittenberg Castle church is discredited. See Iserloh, 1980, p48). His intention was to clarify the church's teaching on indulgences and as there was no official definition at that time he believed he was within the bounds of permissible debate.

The questions he asked in his Ninety-Five Theses were taken up rapidly by many others, indicating widespread unease. Because the subject touched on the financial interests of the Archbishop of Mainz as well as the pope, steps were taken to have Luther accused of heresy. Subsequent proceedings rumbled on through 1518, came to a head in a public Disputation at Leipzig 1519, and resulted in Luther's excommunication 1520 by the papal bull *Exsurge Domine* unless he recanted within sixty days. The grounds for excommunication were items taken from his writings.

The affair was complicated by Frederick of Saxony, who supported Luther, in part as a means of asserting his own independence against Charles V, elected Emperor of the Holy Roman Empire in 1519. For his part Charles V was determined upon retaining his powers over most of Europe and also upon being the champion of the Church.

The inquiries into Luther's writings were far from thorough and it seemed to many in Germany that he had not been given a fair hearing. Charles V therefore agreed to a further examination at the Diet of Worms 1521 before putting into effect the required procedures of excommunication which included treating Luther as an outlaw and destroying his writings. Opinion was divided but Charles V decided to suppress what he regarded as Luther's heresy of setting himself against the church's authority. On his way back to Wittenberg Luther was kidnapped by Frederick of Saxony his protector. He was imprisoned for his own safety in the Wartburg Castle for ten months.

Luther's thought developed in the years between 1511 and 1521. His own spiritual experiences were the starting point but his official examinations and the preparation for them widened the range of his comment. Two of his writings, from 1520, illustrate the sharpness of his criticism and the implications of accepting his arguments (Bettenson, 1943, p269-279).

To the Christian nobility of the German nation (in German) opposes the authority of the pope to whom is attributed all the evils in German society. 'Poor Germans that we are, we have been deceived. We were born to be masters, and we have been compelled to bow the head beneath the yoke of our tyrants and to become slaves.' The nation's wealth is in the hands of the clergy and finds its way to Rome, while the population is deprived of spiritual care. Luther sets out an extensive programme of reform, covering education, poor relief and the control of corrupt finance houses (such as the Fuggers of Augsburg). He argues for the restrictions of payments to Rome, the abolition of clerical celibacy, the release of monastics from their vows, the confiscation of church lands and the simplification of rites and ceremonies. The key Reformation claim to the priesthood of all believers is stated here, based on *1 Peter* 2:9.

The Babylonian Captivity of the Church (in Latin) meant for theologians, criticises the medieval scheme of the seven sacraments and their explanation, based on Aquinas. Luther accepts only three sacraments (baptism, penance, eucharist), later excluding penance. Nothing need be believed about the sacraments which is not expressly stated in scripture. He complains that the Church's attitude has undermined the necessity of faith.

Henry VIII of England wrote an attack on this treatise called *Assertion of the Seven Sacraments,* for which, with some prompting, the pope accorded him the title Defender of the Faith (*Fidei Defensor*, still to be found on coins, in various abbreviations).

While Luther was in seclusion in the Wartburg Castle he began to translate the New Testament into German (it was completed with the Old Testament in 1534). His style was fresh and direct, and the idiomatic German did much to shape the literary form of the language. Luther also composed prayers and hymns and wrote sermons and much of this output was quickly in print and widely read.

The German Reformation (1521-1555)

Charles V, supreme ruler in Germany, also ruled Spain and Austria. Political interests there, conflict with France and quarrels with the pope took him away from Germany. The Edict of Worms 1521 was not enforced and Luther's ideas gained ground.

In 1524-5 there were major uprisings in south and central Germany termed the German Peasants' War. Anti-Lutheran propaganda at the time attributed the unrest to his ideas of equality and freedom for all, but modern research into the social and economic background shows that for one hundred and fifty years there had been sporadic uprisings with appeals to both secular and ecclesiastical rulers to relieve the distress of tax burdens and the poverty caused by the loss of common pastureland. Luther's writings did not incite rebellion but perhaps acted as an accelerator and put new energy into efforts for change. Oberman (1986, p157) notes 'a clearly traceable tone of impatience in the political petitions and polemical pamphlets of the time.' Expectations were raised. Unfortunately there were no competent leaders with military experience and there were many casualties. As failure seemed imminent violence increased, partly in response to the preaching of Müntzer who believed this was the final battle against all evil. Luther was totally opposed to the rebels' use of the gospel to justify their claims and wrote a savage tract 'Against the murdering thieving hordes of peasants.' His abusive language offended many who were equally opposed to the fighting.

There are at least three contemporary comments on the Peasants' War. Erasmus, in 1525, though anxious to see peace restored believed the uprising was primarily against bishops and clergy, though it was against the nobles and princes as well. An ambassador reported from Baden to the regent of the Netherlands also in 1525, that the outcome was uncertain and that it was really civil war. The third account is by Schappeler of Memmingen, one of the peasant leaders who helped to write the Twelve Articles setting out their demands. He is saddened that what began as justifiable resistance to crushing tax burdens has degenerated into unrestrained violence from impatience to satisfy their needs. The Twelve Articles were intended for negotiation but became unconditional demands. (See G. Elton *Renaissance and Reformation 1300-1648*, 1976, p324 for the items listed.)

Though these revolts were put down with severity they affected the poorer people in the cities as well as in the country and the rulers were anxious to avoid further trouble. Luther realised that firm government was essential and his attitude to the peasants lost him the popular enthusiasm he first had. In 1529 at the Diet of Speyer the Catholic rulers tried to prevent any further changes in religion, but other rulers claimed freedom to act according to their conscience, and from this originated the term Protestant.

It had now become necessary to make some provision for congregations which no longer adhered to the Catholic Church. Luther himself at first believed congregations could devise their own liturgies, but the laity were not sufficiently creative or well enough educated to do this. Before long, Lutheran churches were dominated by clergy who were paid by local rulers largely from the proceeds of property confiscated from monasteries. Clergy were allowed to marry, but continued to wear traditional vestments. The bible and preaching became more prominent and teaching was also given through hymns. German was used instead of Latin and some of the prayers modified to reflect Luther's teaching about the eucharist which was celebrated rather less frequently than before. It was believed that these changes were simply rectifying abuses and errors which had grown up in the Catholic Church and the possibility of reconciliation was not ruled out.

Meanwhile Charles V wanted German financial support against Turkish Muslims whose advance along the Danube threatened Vienna. The German Protestant rulers agreed to a meeting at Augsburg in 1530 to discuss this, provided that the religious problems were settled first. To make such an inquiry possible the *Augsburg Confession* of Lutheran belief was drafted by Melancthon. It seemed to suggest that the only differences were in external matters, such as letting the laity have wine as well as bread at communion and permitting the clergy to marry. The outcome was inconclusive, but Charles V began to consider war against the Protestant rulers. He had some success but was not strong enough to enforce his will on all the northern German territories which were now firmly Protestant.

The Peace of Augsburg in 1555 marked the final division of Germany into Protestant and Catholic. Its main significant provision was that the ruler of a territory had the right to decide its religion (*cuius regio, eius et religio*). Church land was secularised and church authority suspended in the Protestant territories. Lutheranism was not formally recognised and, after all the discussion about individual freedom, only the ruler of a territory actually possessed full religious liberty.

From well before Luther's time there had been repeated requests for a general council of the Church. The pope now convened it at Trent, in 1545, in the year Luther died. (See below).

Reformation outside Germany

News of events in the north German territories spread rapidly. Scholars maintained regular correspondence with one another: so, for example, Sir Thomas More knew from Erasmus in 1518 about Luther's Ninety-Five Theses. Students abroad took home information together with copies of Luther's early writing from Froben's printing press in Basle. Traders also transmitted reports of what was happening for there were economic consequences of the German rulers' challenge to Charles V.

In many European countries theologians had pondered the same issues as Luther and been influenced as he had been by humanist writings. They too wished to do away with the corruption of religious institutions and to find a more profound experience of religion. Such people received Luther's writings with interest and were stimulated by them to formulate their own understanding of the Christian faith. As a consequence there was variety in Reformation movements outside Germany and strictly Lutheran Churches were established only in Scandinavia.

Scandinavia

The network of German trading posts in the Baltic countries provided the means of access for missionaries from Lutheran Churches and their teaching found ready acceptance. The Catholic Church was associated with southern European culture which was alien to the north and, in addition, these countries were at the point of establishing their national identity under active and successful rulers. Luther's devotional writings and the New Testament were translated into the vernacular and were popular at all levels of society.

Charles III, who became King of Denmark in 1536, had actually been present at the Diet of Worms and admired Luther. He organised the Danish Reformation and Luther himself was consulted over details. Although the king financed the clergy, schools and hospitals from confiscated church property he was eager to have the remaining revenue to finance the expenses of government. He initiated a similar Reformation in Norway which was then a dependency of Denmark.

In Sweden, Gustavus Vasa began the Reformation by abolishing clergy privileges and taking over church revenues, again glad to have these large sources of income. The situation was complicated by factions among the nobles and social unrest among the poor but the change to a Lutheran form of church was completed gradually. Church leaders were uneasy at too great a dependence upon the monarch and in 1572 negotiated control over the Swedish Lutheran Church. In the next century during the Thirty Years War (1618-1648) Swedish armies in Europe maintained Protestant power in northern Germany as well as in the Baltic.

Switzerland (Zwingli and Calvin)

The Reformation in Zurich was influenced by Ulrich Zwingli (1484-1531). He studied in Vienna and Basle and absorbed many of the humanist ideas of Erasmus. His own theological reflection developed independently though he knew something of Luther's writings and was aware of the indulgence controversy. He became a preacher in Zurich in 1518 and enjoyed the support of the city council which cooperated with his ideas in the religious changes which constituted their Reformation.

Alterations were made gradually. In 1523 revenue from the dissolution of monasteries and from church endowments provided funds for charitable purposes. Churches were greatly altered by the removal of statues and pictures. The Mass was abolished in 1525 after Zwingli's preaching had re-educated people in the new teaching. The city council issued statutory requirements for each of these changes, making a close identification between political, social and religious duties.

Over the years the difference between Zwingli's views and those of Luther became clearer and illustrate some of the divisions which affected the Reformation from the start. Zwingli attached greater importance to preaching the Word of God as a means of generating faith: the sacraments of baptism and eucharist were secondary and were really public demonstrations of belief. He revised the 'Mass' and abolished that name. The Reformation claim to make scripture the sole authority proved to be problematic, for Zwingli differed from Luther over which important texts were to be interpreted literally and which figuratively.

For Zwingli, Reformation meant chiefly the regeneration of the morality of society, with Christ as the example and scripture the code of conduct. He believed in the absolute sovereignty of God with mankind's total dependence, and this is reflected in his assertion that citizens should be obedient to the city council as the representation of divine authority.

There were also radical reformers in Zurich who found the pace of change too slow and who disagreed with Zwingli's close linking of church and civil authority. These reformers have come to be known as Anabaptists because they insisted on a re-baptism to signify adult commitment. They were individualists who refused to conform and were expelled from Zurich as sources of disruption. They scattered around German-speaking countries in northern Europe forming autonomous groups. They had little interest in theological complexities and took no advantage of writing and printing to publicise their ideas. By their very nature they had no organisational structures and were generally unwelcome, suffering persecution and martyrdom.

After Luther, John Calvin (1509-1564) was the most significant Reformation theologian. He had a wide knowledge of classical literature, the Church Fathers and the Bible, largely his own private study. Having accepted the main beliefs of the Reformers, he moved around some of the major cities, such as Basle, and Strasbourg, where he had the opportunity of meeting leading preachers and scholars and of learning what was happening in Germany.

Eventually, in 1541, he settled in Geneva, where the city council wanted to establish a Reformed Church. This was not a simple matter since the people had overthrown the Catholic Church not so much for reasons of devotion and piety as to be rid of the burden of the Duke of Savoy and the bishop. Although Calvin wished the secular authority to support the church he sometimes found interference in ecclesiastical matters went beyond what he thought was justified. For example, the ultimate choice of pastors, teachers elders and deacons was made by the city council who also excommunicated offenders and deprived them of their citizenship.

The aim was to create a Christian community. To this end the preaching of the pastors was regulated and the conduct of the laity closely supervised. The elders inquired into personal behaviour, denouncing cases of gossiping, card-playing, brawling and drunkenness. Repeated offenders were reported to a committee of elders and pastors, and punishments carried out by the magistrates.

In 1559 Calvin founded an Academy for the study of theology, Greek and Hebrew, and biblical exegesis. Many scholars were attracted to it so that standards were high and when they returned home they proved to be important figures in establishing in their own countries Reformed Churches on Calvinist lines.

Calvin never met Luther but he admired him, studied his writings and shared the fundamental beliefs in God's sovereignty, justification by grace through faith, and scripture as the sole source of doctrine. But he belonged to the next generation and saw the necessity of avoiding further division among Reformed Churches and of establishing order and consistency in teaching and administration. His series of enlarged editions of *Institutes of the Christian Religion* (1536, 1539, 1543, 1550, 1559) incorporated his developed thought on the major issues of faith and practice. It has been said that his 'theological system is little more than a brilliant systematisation of Luther's' (Dickens, 1967, p122) but that assessment does not give due weight to the difference made by his own characteristic emphases.

One such emphasis is his teaching on predestination. Like other

Reformers he insists on the absolute sovereignty of God. Sinners are saved irrespective of their merits (whereas with Luther it is despite their faults) and the human mind cannot fathom the mystery of why some are chosen and not others. But for those who are so chosen there are special responsibilities which are to be fulfilled within the Reformed church.

The nature of the Church was a particular concern of Calvin, based on his extensive reading of the early Church Fathers as well as on his earlier legal training. He believed that the Reformed Church was the original universal church purified from later errors. It was characterised by the true preaching of the Word of God and the right administration of the sacraments of baptism and eucharist. Its organisation was divinely laid down in scripture so that there should be one form of church government. In other matters there might be permissible divergence of opinion but there was no need for the fragmentation which had been happening so extensively.

Believing this about the Church, Calvin was not content with limiting his influence to Geneva. Those who went out from his Academy were expected to establish Reformed Churches in their own countries along the lines he set down, and in extensive correspondence he gave further advice on what should be done. He genuinely belived that the Kingdom of God could be established with the founding of a Christian society, where church and state collaborated to reform morals and transform the quality of life at every level. These beliefs were the inspiration of later groups, such as the Pilgrim Fathers, who emigrated to America to set up such a new society.

An implication of his teaching was that governments should be resisted where they did not support Reformed Churches once they were established. In this way, though he could not have foreseen it, Calvin's teaching was behind the religious conflicts in France, Holland, Scotland and England.

A further implication was that where Calvin's teaching took hold, the Reformed Churches became as firmly institutionalised as the Catholic Church they replaced, and relied on the government to supervise religious life and practice, assuming that rulers would be professing Christians.

England and Scotland

The Reformation in England occurred during the reigns of Henry VIII, Edward VI, Mary Tudor and Elizabeth I between 1527 and 1603. Hillerbrand (1975, p112) argues that, as happened elsewhere, the religious decision of the ruler determined the outcome. At the same time there was the interaction of political and social factors, and the influence of humanism from mainland Europe. In the later part of the century examples of Reformed Churches also influenced events.

Between 1527 and 1534 Henry VIII's impatience for a papal dispensation for divorce led to a series of measures which limited the pope's authority in England, restricted money from being sent to Rome and eventually led to the passing of the Act of Supremacy which made the monarch head of the church and state. Religious practice, however, continued much as before and Henry had no wish for Protestant ideas to spread. In 1536 and 1539 Parliament passed Acts for the Dissolution of the Monasteries. It was said they were corrupt, but their wealth was desired to remedy Henry's financial problems. The sale of the property created a group of landowners who were motivated to prevent any return to the Catholic faith. Although many traditional Catholic practices remained, Protestant ideas gained ground through the greater availability of publications from Reformation Europe and the requirement that each parish church should have a Bible in English. The official translation was that of Miles Coverdale, 1539.

During Edward VI's short reign (1547-1553) the first version of the Book of Common Prayer (1549) was revised in 1552 in a Protestant direction. Mary Tudor succeeded (1553-1558) and reversed all the legislation, in the hope of returning the country to the pope's authority. The persecution and execution of about 300 Protestants made her widely unpopular but, at that time, any religious opposition was regarded as a danger to the state. Some historians (eg Hillerbrand, 1975, p133) believe that attempts to get back land which was formerly church property created greater resistance to the restoration of the Catholic faith than religious conviction.

By the time Elizabeth became queen (1558-1603) memories of the Catholic form of religion had faded, and there was no effective Catholic leadership. The monarch's authority over religion was re-established by the Acts of Supremacy and Uniformity. A few further changes in the Prayer Book struck a compromise between Luther's and Zwingli's view of the eucharist, but there was little in the way of formal theological statement apart from drafts of what eventually became the Thirty-Nine Articles of Faith. Elizabeth delayed assent to these until 1571, a year after her formal excommunication by the pope.

In the second half of the sixteenth century there was growing discontent among Protestant groups in England. Some had returned from their exile during Mary's reign, bringing with them experience of Reformed Churches in Germany and Switzerland. These had seemed attractive because they were well organised along reformed lines and seemed effective in their social impact. They were also grounded in well-argued theological principles. By contrast the religious life in England remained full of un-reformed traditions – in ritual, in the inferior status of preaching, in the observance of saints' days and above all in the superior wealth and status of the bishops. Gradually small groups of dissenters withdrew into private meetings, having failed in their efforts to modify the official church. Where they made public protests they were firmly suppressed, to maintain stability in government.

In Scotland, support for Protestant thought gained ground slowly in a political situation complicated by division among the nobles and competing alliances with France and England. In the early part of the sixteenth century the country was close to civil war. The dominant figure was John Knox (1505-1572) who was attracted to Lutheran doctrine in the 1520s and who studied in Geneva at Calvin's Academy 1547-1549. He returned as a committed Calvinist. He was totally convinced of his mission, but was a fanatical church leader rather than a theologian. His manner was fiery and uncouth so that Samuel Johnson called him one of the 'ruffians' of the Reformation.

In 1558 he took issue with Mary Queen of Scots for retaining her Catholic faith and practice and asserted that loyalty was no longer due to her. The Scottish Parliament in 1560 resolved to abolish the authority and jurisdiction of the pope and the Mass was banned. A Confession of Faith and Doctrine was drawn up by Knox along Calvinist lines but it was not formally approved until 1567 and it was some time before Reformed practices became widespread.

Catholic Reform and Counter Reformation

It is not true that Catholic reform came only after, or as a response to the Protestant challenge. There were moves to reform the Curia at the Fifth Lateran Council (1512-1517), though much remained to be done. Several of the religious orders carried out a thorough overhaul of their houses and tightened discipline. A few new orders were founded to meet new demands. For example, the Theatines were formed in 1524 with the explicit aim of improving standards among priests in the conduct of the liturgy and in the quality of preaching and pastoral care.

In Spain particularly there was a vigorous movement to make bishops take their duties more seriously. An impressive lead was given by the Archbishop of Toledo, Cardinal Ximenes de Cisneros (1495-1517) who was a strict disciplinarian of his clergy. He founded the University of Alcala as a centre of humanist learning and of the study of the Church Fathers. He was instrumental in the production of the Complutensian Polyglot Bible with the Old Testament printed in three parallel columns – the Septuagint (Greek) version, the Latin Vulgate and the Hebrew. He also ordered a Greek New Testament to be printed.

A few years later another Spaniard, Ignatius Loyola (1491-1556) founded the Society of Jesus (1540). His life-span almost coincided with that of Luther, though the two did not meet and it is believed that Ignatius did not read any of Luther's writings. Both had transforming religious experiences but Ignatius believed himself called to help others to inward renewal within the Church of his day. His book *The Spiritual Exercises* is still widely used (often by non-Catholics). The scope of Jesuit activity was to be world-wide and its members, in addition to the usual vows of poverty, chastity and obedience, took a fourth, availability for apostolic mission wherever the pope desired them to work. Once established their numbers grew rapidly. They undertook distant missions in Asia and South America but in Europe concentrated on scholarship and higher education. The schools and colleges they founded proved to be a strong force for reform within the Church. They also built many churches in the Baroque style in Italy and South Germany, transforming the atmosphere of worship from medieval to modern and providing for the emotional response of the laity as well as for preaching.

Successive popes were under pressure to call a general council of the Church, even before Luther asked for one to examine the errors of which he was accused. But they were wary of councils. At Constance (1414-1418) and Basle (1431) the authority of papal over council decree had been contested. It was still an important issue at the Council of Ferrara-Florence (1438-1439), the final episode in the Great Schism between eastern and western churches (see previous chapter). Such issues seemed more immediately important than what Leo X called 'a squabble among monks.'

The conflicting views and ambitions of the Emperor, Charles V and Francis I of France has also to be taken into account. By 1545 when Paul III had decided upon a council, the Emperor was opposed to it, convinced that its decisions would finally wreck any chance of religious reconciliation in Germany, whereas earlier it was Francis I who had objected, fearing that a solution to the Protestant problem would strengthen his rival. Further delays were caused by arguments over location (Trent was eventually agreed being in the Emperor's domain but also in Italy) and procedure (solved by taking issues of doctrine and discipline in parallel). Members of the council required permission from their local rulers to travel abroad and the council eventually opened several months late because so few had arrived on time. These details show that calling a council was not an easy matter.

The Council of Trent met in three sessions. The first, 1545-1548, focussed on the German situation. The pope, not present in person, operated through legates and the representatives from other countries were in constant communication with their respective rulers, so that political as well as religious considerations were never far from mind. Theological advisers from the Dominican, Franciscan and Augustinian schools of thought introduced the debates. It was decreed that the canon of scripture, including the Greek apocryphal books already part of the Vulgate, was a source of revelation to be reverenced equally with apostolic tradition (though 'apostolic' was interpreted more narrowly by some than by others). The decree on justification was a lengthy and detailed exposition of the subject. 'It defined the responsibility of grace for justification in all its stages, its nature as sanctification and renewal of the inner man, the necessity of preparation, and the importance of faith in the process of justification; the increase of justification, its restoration and the possibility of merit; and eternal life as grace and reward' (Jedin 1980, p470). [It has been said that if such a comprehensive formulation of doctrine had been made early in the sixteenth century religious unity would have been preserved. The problem was reviewed and a reconciling re-statement made in the report of ARCIC II *Salvation and the Church* 1987 (See Section on Second Vatican Council). It was shown that theologians had interpreted the Greek-Latin words differently: 'to make righteous' (Catholic) 'to pronounce righteous' (Protestant)].

The second session, 1551-1552, confirmed the number of sacraments as seven and defined each of them. 'It defined the Real Presence and the notion of transubstantiation as *suitable* for designating the substantial change and condemned the teaching that Christ is present only at the moment of reception' (Jedin, 1980, p477). Here, as elsewhere, the wording was carefully chosen to allow for diversity of opinion within the Catholic Church (see Jedin, 1980, who has studied the minutes of the discussions which became available only this century.) Stricter discipline for bishops was discussed and also reforms of the Curia, but the pope reserved the right to organise these himself.

So far nothing had binding force until the pope gave formal approval. In the next ten years there were three popes. The most important, Paul IV (1555-1559) refused to re-convene the Council. Politics again intruded with the uncertainty caused by the abdication of the Emperor, Charles V in 1556. The pope acted harshly in an attempt to halt the advance of Protestant ideas. He set up a Roman Inquisition (greatly hated) and re-activated the Index of Forbidden Books (1558, meant to be temporary but not abolished until 1978). The list of banned works included translations of the bible, all the writings of the Reformers and also of Erasmus, editions of the Early Fathers and all the publications of 61 printers, 14 of them from Basle. Peter Canisius, 1559, said 'Even the best Catholics disapprove of such rigour.'

The third and final session of the Council of Trent, 1562-1563, was convened by Pius IV who surrounded himself with distinguished reformers. There was increased urgency because in France Calvinism had become strong, and from Spain there was pressure to activate the earlier decisions of the Council. The great need for improved pastoral care which was behind much of the early Lutheran criticism was met by regulations affecting bishops. Some, inevitably, were required for administrative work in the Curia, but for the rest there were substantial penalties for not being in residence. They were required to establish seminaries for the preparation of priests and their authority was strengthened by limiting interference from the Curia. But the relation between bishops and the bishop of Rome (i.e the pope) was not defined.

The decrees were signed by more than 200 cardinals, archbishops, bishops, abbots and generals of religious orders, and ratified by Pius IV 1564. For the next forty years, successive popes ensured reform and regeneration by publication of the decrees as far afield as Mexico and Goa, by organising visits to check on bishops, by modernising the Curia, by establishing theological colleges in Rome and by rehousing the Vatican library. Among the great reforming bishops was Charles Borromeo of Milan (1565-1584) who renewed the spiritual life of his diocese, making personal visits even to remote Alpine villages. His life and writings were studied and edited by Pope John XXIII and helped to form his ideas of how regeneration of the church could come about in the twentieth century (see next chapter).

Conclusion

Hillerbrand (1975, p179) says 'The Reformation was a spiritual movement of elementary religious forces that sought to replace a sophisticated church and religion with a handful of simple affirmations.' But by the second half of the sixteenth century both Catholic and Protestant religious leaders were trying to overcome widespread ignorance of the Christian faith and to promote a deeper spirituality. Their methods were similar. Parallel to the decrees of the Council of Trent, Protestants produced 'confessions' of faith and statements of church order. Both Catholics and Protestants printed catechisms and textbooks to ensure their people were better informed and both established institutions for the improved preparation of the clergy.

A negative result of this activity was a hardening of divisions, not only between Catholic and Protestant but between Protestants. Denominations were defined by distinctions, and statements of belief tended to disregard common ground. As a result there was often a narrowing of horizons and impoverishment in religious faith. There remained a lingering belief in the one-ness of the Christian Church, so that the conviction of each denomination became the test of the true faith, and opponents were seen as heretics. In mainland Europe, following the Peace of Augsburg, 1555, most territories had only one form of church; but in England, and particularly in the seventeenth century, there was a proliferation of Protestant groups. This remains a distinguishing feature. In 1990 *Churches Together in England* was inaugurated with 20 member churches (see *Reflections* edit. V. Nichols, 1986, Inter-Church Process). In the twentieth century the divisions of the Reformation which arose from so many inter-related causes are being reconsidered and for the first time it is realised how many of them can be attributed to misunderstanding.

CHAPTER NINE

MEETING TWENTIETH CENTURY CHALLENGES

Between the Reformation and the twentieth century there have been major cultural and social changes, an expansion of technological and scientific knowledge, and horizons widened by exploration and colonialism. Nationalism and imperialism, industrialisation and capitalism, revolution and democracy, improved education and communications have all, in their way, affected Christianity.

The intellectual movement known as the Enlightenment, encouraged freedom of inquiry and put reason in the highest place among human attributes. Existing biblical interpretation was challenged, but what at first seemed destructive opened the way for a richer understanding of scripture. In the Roman Catholic Church this exercise of reason applied to the whole range of doctrine (called Modernism), came at a moment when papal territorial power collapsed and the Curia became very sensitive about perceived challenges to its authority. There followed a period of considerable restriction on Catholic scholarship with insistence on the unquestioning acceptance of Rome's pronouncements. Other denominations felt threatened by the increasing secularism of society, initiated by the French Revolution which attempted to overthrow all existing forms of traditional authority, and particularly religious control of any kind.

Alongside this narrowing of Christian influence in Europe there was a remarkable expansion of missionary activity, primarily in Africa and India but also in the Far East and in South America. Areas of work tended to be related to colonial dependency and to trading interests, but those who ventured into distant lands were motivated by the desire to evangelise and were convinced that they had a superior culture to transmit. In North America emigrants sought both religious and political independence and Christian principles combined with democratic ideals have shaped the subsequent history of religion there. Over the years insistence on the individual's freedom of belief and conscience tended to encourage numerous sects and, sometimes, an entrenched opposition to modern biblical scholarship.

In the twentieth century Christianity has maintained itself and responded to the situations which have developed out of the preceding centuries. In the western world, at the beginning of the century the churches seemed to be out-of-touch with changes in society and had yet to come to terms with the challenge of Marxism. Now all denominations have tried to take serious notice of the cultural world in which they operate. Perhaps the most dramatic example of this is the refreshing breeze allowed to blow through the Roman Catholic Church by the work of the Second Vatican Council. The impact of this has been world-wide, and among the outcomes, a tentative but promising encounter with the Orthodox Church, other Christian denominations and, to some extent, other religious faiths.

Nowadays most denominations show interest in one another, an interest reinforced by the experience of missionaries who find their work hindered by division. Secularism has drawn Christians to stand together to affirm fundamental agreements of far greater importance than their differences. This concern for unity is known as the ecumenical movement, at one level directed to unity among Christians but also, in a more hesitant way, to the unity of human beings everywhere.

In this chapter attention is given to two major examples of renewal and reconciliation: the World Council of Churches and the Second Vatican Council. In the twenty-first century further chapters will need to be written about both of these for their impact and consequences are in no way past history.

The World Council of Churches

The origins of the World Council of Churches (WCC) are to be found in three important ecumenical movements of the early twentieth century. A world missionary conference was held in Edinburgh in 1910, and, as a result the *International Missionary Council* was founded in 1920, largely from the efforts of John R. Mott and J. H. Oldham. In 1925 there was a *Universal Conference on Life and Work* held in Stockholm, promoted by Archbishop Nathan Söderblom of Uppsala. It was concerned with finding ways in which Christians could support each other in influencing society, for example in industry, education and international affairs. Then, in 1927, there was the *First*

World Conference on Faith and Order held in Lausanne, under the inspiration of Bishop Brent, bishop of the Philippine Islands and Western New York.

The 'Life and Work' and 'Faith and Order' movements both held conferences in 1937 and agreed to plan a world council which would combine both movements. The sense of urgency for joining forces came from the European situation which was dominated by the misery of unemployment, by the oppression of tyrannical governments and by the fear of war. Fulfilment of this project was delayed by the outbreak of the Second World War but the WCC was inaugurated soon afterwards in Amsterdam, 1948. The International Missionary Council did not join the WCC until 1961, partly because it was an association of missionary societies, rather than churches, but also because of fears that its missionary character would be overshadowed by the concerns of the large organisation. In reality these three main elements of the WCC have interacted productively, and each has enriched and enhanced the whole.

The original basis was expressed briefly as follows: *The WCC is a fellowship of churches which accept the Lord Jesus Christ as God and Saviour.* By the third world assembly at New Delhi, in 1961, and with the enlargement of membership this was considered inadequate. The constitution now states the basis as:

> *The WCC is a fellowship of churches which confess the Lord Jesus Christ as God and Saviour according to the scriptures and therefore seek to fulfil together their common calling to the glory of the one God, Father, Son and Holy Spirit.*

This basis is not a creed, but it functions as a definition of the nature of the Council and indicates the limits of membership.

The additions satisfied or reassured members. Evangelical groups wanted the reference to scripture and the more explicit trinitarian phrasing was important to the Orthodox churches.

The functions and purposes of the Council are stated in the Constitution. At the head is the statement that the goal is *visible unity in one faith and in one eucharistic fellowship expressed in worship and in common life in Christ, and to advance towards that unity in order that the world may believe.* This remains an ideal and what it means is discussed again and again at the major assemblies, each time with an enlargement of meaning. At New Delhi, 1961, the unity of 'all Christians in all places' was understood to mean all Christians, regardless of race or class, in all neighbourhoods, work places and nations. At Uppsala, 1968, the goal of ecumenical unity was interpreted in its original sense of the whole inhabited earth, and to further this objective the Programme to Combat Racism was set up.

Unity does not mean uniformity, but the legtimate limits of diversity are still vigorously debated. At the most recent assembly in Canberra, 1991, any complacency over coexistence in division was deplored. Diversity has both positive and negative aspects. If it means retaining national and ethnic identities it is to be welcomed as enriching everybody, but if it means exclusion and division it is to be rejected. The scope of unity has now been extended to include the whole of creation. 'A reconciled and renewed creation is the goal of the church's mission – God unites all things in Christ' (Canberra Report 1991).

The Council is a *fellowship* of churches. It is not a superchurch nor a federation of churches, nor a substitute for a united church. It has no authority over member churches which remain autonomous within their own traditions. Its pronouncements are often regarded as influential internationally but they come from the Council and are not necessarily a true reflection of the views of constituent members.

The main groups of non-members are the Roman Catholic Church, and a number of Pentecostal, Independent and Evangelical Churches.

Since 1961 there have been Roman Catholic official observers at the assembly and since Uppsala, 1968, a number of Roman Catholic theologians have been appointed as full members of the Commission on Faith and Order. There have also been other forms of collaboration, most notably in the preparation for the Week of Prayer for Christian Unity held either in January or between Ascension and Pentecost. In 1969 Pope Paul VI visited the WCC headquarters in Geneva. The Joint Working Group, set up after Uppsala, reported in 1972 that there were no theologicial, ecclesiastical or canonical obstacles to applying for membership of the Council but it was not thought that the time was right. There would in any case be considerable problems because of the large numbers of Roman Catholics throughout the world. Ecumenical collaboration is encouraged, for example in the United Kingdom, but there are major difficulties for reconciliation in Ireland.

Many Pentecostal, Independent and Evangelical Churches,

especially those in the western world, withhold their support for a number of reasons. They are suspicious simultaneously of communist, Roman Catholic and liberal influences in the Council's projects. They are very often hostile towards political and social involvement, or simply uninterested. They do not consider that a world organisation will contribute to individual conversion and to some extent reject the ecumenical movement because they regard it as a human effort to attain unity.

Although these groups do not completely agree with one another they tend to hold in common a belief in the literal inspiration and infallibility of scripture and require believers' baptism. Collaboration and dialogue with other Christians seem to them a denial of the faith as they understand it, but at the Canberra assembly in 1991 it was reported that some Pentecostal and Evangelical groups have begun to consult with one another, for example in Latin America.

Organisation

World assemblies of the Council are held at approximately seven yearly intervals and are attended by official delegates from the member churches. Numbers have expanded over the years from 150 churches in 1948 to 320 in 1991.

1948	Amsterdam	Man's disorder and God's design
1954	Evanston	Jesus Christ, the hope of the world
1961	New Delhi	Jesus Christ, the light of the world
1968	Uppsala	Behold I make all things new
1975	Nairobi	Jesus Christ frees and unites
1983	Vancouver	Jesus Christ, the life of the world
1991	Canberra	Come Holy Spirit – renew the whole creation

The infrastructure of committees has been reorganised over the years to meet the Council's increasing size and range of work. Between the assemblies, a Central Committee carries out the Council's instructions, working through an Executive Committee. In 1991, a new organisational structure was proposed with five administrative centres responsible for the items listed overleaf.

I *Unity and Renewal*
Faith and Order: search for visible unity
Search for Inclusive Community
Renewal through Worship and Spirituality
Ecumenical Formation and Theological Education
Theological Reflection and Interfaith Dialogue
Reflection on Justice, Peace and the Integrity of Creation

II *Mission, Education and Witness*
Evangelism
Unity in Mission
Supporting the education tasks of the churches
Mission to challenge unjust structures
Gospel and culture
Theological Significance of Religions
Healing and Transformation

III *Justice, Peace and Creation*
Justice, Peace and the Integrity of Creation: a Conciliar Process
Theological, Ethical, Socio-economic and Ecological Analysis
Economic Justice
Peace ministries and Conflict Resolution
Indigenous Peoples, Land Rights and Racism
Human Rights
Concerns and Perspectives of Women
Concern and Perspectives of Youth
Education on Issues of Justice, Peace and Creation
Churches' Response to International Affairs
Communication as Power

IV *Sharing and Service*
Solidarity by Sharing Resources
Service of Human Need
Comprehensive Diakonia
Development of Human Resources
New Models for Sharing and Service
Biblical and Theological Analysis

V *General Secretariat*
Management and Finance
Church and Ecumenical Relations
Interreligious Relations
Communications
Programme Coordination

Such a long list of subjects covered by the WCC is evidence of its growing complexity. Substantial reports are produced in preparation for the next assembly and in other ways to publicise the Council's work and encourage a wider appreciation of ecumenical issues. One such report is *Baptism, Eucharist and Ministry* (1982) which is being studied by churches world-wide as a foundation for agreement on these issues.

The administrative base is in Geneva where the General Secretary has a staff of about 300. Their work included the preparation of publicity material and the production of information for member churches. Several official languages are used (e.g. English, French, German) but there is a quantity of work for translators and interpreters. The General Secretariat also maintains a network of relations with other ecumenical bodies. Examples are national councils of churches, YMCA, and YWCA, and the World Christian Communions of Lutherans, Reformed Churches, Methodists, Baptists, Anglicans and United Churches.

At Bossey, near Geneva, there is an Ecumenical Institute, which provides training courses and is the base for numerous conferences and seminars. This was officially opened in 1946.

The funding for all of this comes from the contributions of member churches and specific projects have also been funded by government or other agencies. In 1986 the Council's total expenditure was about 37 million Swiss francs. In that year 42 per cent of income was spent on the work of what was then called 'Justice and Service.'

Almost from the beginning there have been criticisms of increasing bureaucracy and complaints that the Ecumenical Centre in Geneva is remote from Third World countries. Any large organisation attracts this sort of criticism and there are continued attempts to make improvements. It is recognised that there is no one right structure and modifications will continue to be made to serve the Council's needs.

The impact of expansion

The formation of the WCC owed much to British Church leaders and in the early years the major influences were European and North American. The balance began to shift from 1961 when, at the New Delhi assembly, new members were admitted from countries in the southern hemisphere. Many of these had recently attained their independence from colonial status, for example in South America,

Africa, Asia and the Caribbean. Further additions have increased the numbers of churches from the Developing World. The effects of this have been responsible for a number of changes within the WCC, and not simply in more complex organisation to accommodate large numbers.

The expansion of Unit II 'Justice and Service' and the titles of its working groups illustrate the difference made by the membership from countries of the Developing World. For the most part these churches know first hand the problems of poverty and oppression. Frequently their governments are unstable, corrupt or simply overwhelmed by their difficulties. Christian churches are often isolated from one another, so that issues of differing beliefs are of little significance compared with the struggles of survival. The locating of world assemblies in New Delhi (1961) and Nairobi (1975) enabled delegates from affluent countries to see for themselves difficulties which seem less acute when they are only read about in reports. As a result, the Council has aimed at the mobilisation of the whole people of God to overcome these threats to human dignity and well-being and to take a stand against injustice.

But not all members have approved. Financial provision for the projects of 'Justice and Service' inevitably comes mainly from the wealthy countries of the northern hemisphere and sometimes they do not agree with what is being done at their expense. In some instances there is a conflict of interest between national policies and the Council's aims in the developing countries.

At a deeper level there is perhaps tension between the descendants of the founding ecumenical movements: 'Faith and Order', which concentrated on doctrinal matters, and 'Life and Work', oriented towards the Christian transformation of society. From time to time members have been reminded that Christianity requires both approaches, but there is no total reconciliation of these emphases. It seems that the division has run through many of the member churches so that within any one church there are likely to be those who do not want involvement in social and political issues and those who want an even more radical approach to matters of justice and service.

At the organisational level there has been difficulty in assimilating Developing World representation into the major committees and secretariat. The committees use western-style democratic and parliamentary procedures with a follow-up system of reports. Those without this kind of experience are often not able to operate effectively within such a framework. Many people are excluded because they lack the linguistic skills and technical expertise which would enable them to fit into the central organisation or to participate in policy forming discussion and debate. And if they have acquired this kind of education they may have ceased to be truly representative of their own people. Every effort is made to overcome these difficulties and to make use of the insights and experience of Developing World representatives.

Many of the Christian churches in Africa and Asia and India are minority groups co-existing with major religions such as Islam Hinduism and Buddhism. A better understanding of the position of these churches has awakened others to the necessity of improving relations between the major faiths. This realisation has coincided with the development of multi-cultural societies in many countries which have had a long-established Christian tradition. Missionaries have always been brought into some sort of relationship with other faiths but there is now in the Council a different mode of approach.

'Unity and Renewal' has a working group on Interfaith Dialogue. The term 'dialogue' implies openness towards the other, the treatment of the other as an equal partner and a willingness to change. Formerly, in a missionary context, the talking did not take account of the possibility of authentic knowledge of God present in the other's faith. The work of the Holy Spirit is now more widely recognised as present everywhere, and not restricted to the Christ event. Consequently there is truth to be found, recognised and understood in other faiths. 'Dialogue is an authentic form of Christian witness and ministry' (Canberra, 1991). With this change of emphasis, the ecumenical movement is coming towards new possibilities of reconciliation and towards a fresh interpretation of the Christian faith in a multi-religious world.

Here again there have been difficulties. For some this dialogue signifies a weakening of the missionary endeavour and even carries a threat of syncretism. There is the fear of a loss of Christian identity (though the reverse is the most usual experience). This anxiety goes along with doubts about the liturgical and other differences introduced by people of other cultures in the process of expressing their Christian faith in their own terms. The problem is to distinguish accurately between the essential faith and the traditional forms of expression, shaped as these have been by the Greek and Roman influences of the western world. At Canberra 1991, concern was expressed over what some regarded as 'an alarming mishmash of Christianity and paganism.' The interaction between theology and cultural context appears to be an increasingly urgent subject for discussion.

On their side, the Developing World countries have found it hard to come to terms with the position of those who recommend the simple lifestyle of discipleship while enjoying the benefits and comforts of sophisticated modern technological society. They also wonder how far the acquisitive materialism and consumerism of western civilisation is ultimately destructive of human welfare.

Problems and Prospects

Tensions between member churches persist, perhaps for underlying and not always conscious theological reasons. An early attitude was caricatured as 'Sit, brothers of the Son of Man, and leave it all to God.' Somewhat unfairly this attitude has been associated with the early theology of Karl Barth and his followers, though he himself changed his stance in the 1930s in face of the German political situation which threatened the integrity of the church. In the 1960s an important theological influence was that of Bonhoeffer with his emphasis on meeting the needs of the world as these are perceived in each generation. In the 1990s, traditional theology has been unsettled by a Spirit-centred theology of creation and since Canberra, 1991, misgivings have been voiced over the new emphasis on creation spirituality.

Dissatisfaction with the Council is expressed by the impatient: they say there are too many speeches and not enough action. At the assembly in Uppsala 1968 there were demonstrations by youth movements who complained about the number of earlier decisions which had not been implemented. One of these dated from the Lund Faith and Order Conference of 1952 where it was resolved that churches should act together except where conscience compels them to act separately. In 1991 at Canberra it was recognised that this principle is still not acted upon.

Frequently there seems to be a gulf between the consultations of the Council and the concerns of the member churches. Do local congregations of member churches make any attempt to put into practice the ideas their representatives are expounding or supporting in Council debates? Sometimes they show very little interest in them, either to agree or to disagree. This neglect is justified by the argument that local demands must first be met and that energy, time and money are limited. And for some the vast problems of the world seem overwhelming, and there is a sense of helplessness which results in withdrawal into restricted objectives or doctrinal rigidity.

Flawed communications can also be blamed for the 'involvement gap' between member churches and the world ecumenical movement. Information put out from the centre in Geneva may not reach its destination because it is not presented in a suitable form. Church leaders may not report intelligibly to the local congregations nor keep them up-to-date with new developments. The most widely received information comes from the media. Controversial elements are picked out, and these are often political or social matters, giving a distorted representation of the Council's total range of concern.

But these problems can scarcely be avoided in such a large and diverse organisation. Valid criticisms help the movement to be alert to its own shortcomings and to work for improvement in its arrangements. It is too extreme a judgment to claim as some have that the institution has outlived its usefulness or to be sure that it is heading in the wrong direction.

The ecumenical movement developed in Europe between the two world wars and at first it seemed to some to be 'a pale religious reflection of the League of Nations' (Hastings, 1986, p305). It gained strength and purpose from the desire to support churches caught up in a worsening international political conflict. The Life and Work Conference message in 1937 stated 'The first duty of the Church and its greatest service to the world, is that it be in very deed the Church'. Together the churches could speak more forcefully about the ills of society and perhaps exert greater authority than by making separate approaches to governments. To some extent this hope has been fulfilled. Today the Council supports agencies such as the United Nations and the International Court of Justice in their work towards greater international justice and peace. There is room for all such initiatives in tackling the world's problems and the churches have given an important lead in preparing public opinion and in being able to rise above narrow national objectives.

Sociologists have pointed to internal economic benefits from the ecumenical movement. In the western world, where Christian belief has declined in the twentieth century, it seemed sensible to share reduced resources and utilise clergy more efficiently. In post-war rebuilding and in the new towns, ecumenical team ministries have been set up and since 1948 there have also been examples of church unions. In the United Kingdom the United Reformed Church is composed of former congregational and Presbyterian Churches (from 1972) and the Association of Churches of Christ (from 1981).

Methodists came together in stages from 1906 to 1932 and there were protracted Anglican-Methodist consultations from 1946. These resulted in a final agreed scheme in 1968 but reunion foundered when the Anglican vote fell short of the 75 per cent majority required. Methodist and the United Reformed Church are currently exploring the possibility of union.

Perhaps the most significant instance of church union was that of Anglicans, Methodists, Presbyterians and Congregationalists in the Church of South India, in 1947. They came together as minority Christian groups in a mainly Hindu society (though there are also numerous Catholics in the area and a strong Old Malabar Church). Later this union of churches was extended to include those of North India, Pakistan and Bangladesh.

There have been ecumenical consultations with the Roman Catholic Church since Vatican II (see below). The changed situation in Eastern Europe has affected relations with the Orthodox Churches as groups following the Latin or Byzantine rite try to re-establish themselves now that state persecution has ended. The immediate problem is that of regaining property which the state had confiscated and transferred to the Orthodox Churches. In the Middle East Oriental Catholic Churches (eg Armenian, Chaldean) also have difficult relations with the Orthodox Churches. Though the Roman Catholic Church does not belong to the World Council of Churches, Eastern and Oriental Orthodox Churches do so that the Council is necessarily interested in helping towards resolving the problems. The Canberra Report 1991 points to the risk of the church being a divisive rather than a unifying force in these new circumstances.

As the world situation alters so the WCC has to meet new challenges. In some ways the early emphasis was upon internal relationships, natural and necessary when membership was expanding. Time was needed to become acquainted in order to speak and to act together. There were unrealistic expectations of resolving long-standing doctrinal differences within the space of a few years but these hopes have been replaced by a more pragmatic intention of doing whatever can be done now, especially in challenging the world with Christian values. In the local and national counterparts of the WCC there seems to be a replication of the same pattern of development. Early on there was enthusiasm for worshipping together and visiting each other's churches. Now that this experience has been sampled there is beginning to be greater emphasis placed on collaboration in projects for the benefit of society as a whole. It is increasingly realised that there is already the unity of a Christian way of life and that this unity can command respect and exert influence.

The Second Vatican Council

When Pope John XXIII announced in January 1959 that there was to be an Ecumenical Council of the Church there was some astonishment. What was it to be about?

The two most recent councils had apparently settled all possible questions. The Council of Trent (1545-1563) was a reforming council and had dealt with justifiable criticisms of the Church as well as with the controversial issues associated with Luther and his supporters. The First Vatican Council (1870) had defined the authority of the pope to make statements on matters of faith and morals without the need to consult the Church as a whole. The permanent ecclesiastical civil service, the Curia, was available to advise and, if need be, to check individual popes. Everything was under control.

What Pope John really had in mind was only gradually understood. He thought the Council could 'let some fresh air into the Church.' The word *aggiornamento* came to be used. It means 'bringing up to date.' What it meant in terms of the Council is more complex. There was to be a return to the sources, a rediscovery of the faith and of the Church's traditions, and an interpretation of them in harmony with the modern world. He had already spoken of this in 1957 when still the Patriarch of Venice. 'Holy Church who is ever youthful wants to be in a position to understand the diverse circumstances of life so that she can adapt, correct, improve and be filled with fervour.'

The need for renewal had been observed by the Pope from an early stage in his career. He saw the Church damaged by its hostility to all modern forms of intellectual inquiry. He thought that dubious scholarship should be confronted by better scholarship whereas the tendency had been to silence or ignore innovative theologians. This policy had resulted in the Church's growing isolation from the contemporary world and in a reduced understanding of their faith by many Catholics. It also prevented the Church from exerting a beneficial influence on society. Individual bishops, priests, and theologians had endeavoured to counter such isolation and their work proved to be of immense value as a foundation for Council documents.

Pope John XXIII

John XXIII was pope for less than five years. His election at the age of
seventy-six indicated that he was thought of as 'the transitional
pope', 'a safe elderly conservative.' His past career as a papal
diplomat had taken him to Belgrade, Istanbul, Paris and Venice and,
though respected as a pastor, he was generally taken to be politically
naive, 'an old buffer in carpet slippers.' A more perceptive
evaluation was made by the Archbishop of Paris in 1949.

> He was always friendly and understanding, and sought to
> smooth out difficult problems, but when action was needed, he
> did not lack decisiveness and firmness of character. His
> goodness was not soggy but strong. Furthermore, he could be
> subtle, perspicacious and far-sighted, and I could give plenty of
> examples of the way he slipped through the grasp of those who
> sought to exploit him.
> (Quoted by Hebblethwaite, 1984, p227)

Some months before his election he had to make an official speech at
Lourdes. He prefaced it like this. 'It is rather long but be patient. I
will read and you will listen. Thus we shall do honour to the
Madonna who loves us. If at a certain point you grow too weary,
make a sign to me and I will stop, and you can read the speech
tomorrow in the newspapers.' His goodness, piety, humanity and
humour shine through this and many other stories told about him.
He surprised the Vatican gardeners by chatting to them, saying that
he belonged only to 'the fat men's party.' He simplifed the
customary style of referring to the pope. Again and again he would
say, in conciliatory fashion, 'I am your brother Joseph.' Because of
his unassuming manner one bishop later said 'we could be forgiven
for not having suspected that he was a saint and a man prepared to
trust and act on his grace-enlightened intuition.'

Although he was already ill in 1962 and died in June 1963 Pope
John's influence on the Council can hardly be exaggerated, but it was
exerted quietly through personal contacts, through his opening
speech to the Council on 11 October 1962 and through the encyclical
Pacem in Terris (Peace on earth) published deliberately on Maundy
Thursday 11 April 1963. Some of our information about his role has
become known only in recent years with the publication of memoirs
and papers not available in the period immediately following the
Council.

The opening address to the Council set the tone for later sessions. The Pope had previously spoken of the need 'to discern the signs of the times' and now he scolded the prophets of doom who saw nothing good in modern times. On the contrary, 'Divine Providence is leading us to a new order of human relations.' The Church's best way of counteracting error was not by condemnation but by Christian charity. The Church must work towards the unity both of the whole Christian family and the whole human family. 'The Council now beginning rises in the Church like daybreak, a forerunner of most splendid light. It is now only dawn.'

The influence of these words soon became apparent and also after his death, because in the course of debate and controversy, those who were consistently arguing for thoroughgoing renewal could quote again and again from this opening speech, whereas those of a conservative and reactionary tendency could find nothing in it to support their viewpoint.

His encyclical *Pacem in Terris* has been called his last will and testament. It was written when he knew he was dying, and it articulates many of the major themes found later in the Council's Pastoral Constitution on the Church in the Modern World (*Gaudium et Spes*).

The rights of every human person are laid out in a fresh way. They include the right to religious freedom, national self-determination and democratic forms of government. There is encouragement to be active in politics, which was a departure from the Church's nineteenth century teaching. In developing these points the encyclical envisages cooperation between Church and state in a pluralist society. Some aspects of the modern world are praised, such as the achievements of science. Other advances singled out for mention are improved social conditions for working people, the increasing emancipation of women and the decline of imperialism. References to the positive features of society were not then typical of the Church's assessment of the world but their implications were part of the subsequent debates on renewal.

The Pope did not live to open the Second Session of the Council but he wrote to the bishops asking them to give priority to the study of the draft documents being sent out and to comment on them in detail. The bishops were to take the initiative, he said.

The Council

The Council met in four annual sessions (1962-1965). There was a larger number of bishops than had ever met before (2600) of whom 800 came from outside Europe. There were about 400 theologians and experts in attendance and by the fourth session there were 52 lay members, about half of whom were women. There were non-Catholic observers from the Russian Orthodox Church and most other major Christian churches. Sometimes informal conversation between Council members and observers influenced the wording of official statements in the direction of reconciliation. In adding to this wide representation the media were actively encouraged to report the Council and discuss the issues so that maximum publicity was given to what was happening.

The sixty days of the first session decided what kind of Council it was to be. The conservative members of the Curia at first tried to limit discussion by presenting prepared documents for the bishops' amendment of superficial details. In a quite unexpected way individual bishops challenged the pre-arranged procedures and a secret ballot made it clear that they were determined on a more radical approach. Pope John Paul II (as Bishop of Krakow) was among those who intervened with arguments which demonstrated the need for thorough discussion of the issues. It then became apparent that further sessions would be needed and the Pope, although grievously disappointed that he would not live to see the end of the Council, supported those who said the bishops needed more time to get to know each other. He thought that the 'sharply divergent views' illustrated 'the holy liberty that the children of God enjoy in the Church.' (An archbishop there translated this as 'the children of God who were able to slide down the banisters in the house of the Lord.')

In succeeding sessions there was continued openness of discussion and argument as the bishops worked to find ways of representing the Church faithfully to the modern world. They had first to look at themselves. One who was there has remarked on the salutary effect of two and a half thousand bishops having to elbow their way through to the coffee bars arguing with each other just as students do. For a time they were at liberty to express themselves quite freely without having to be on their best behaviour as public figures.

The Council did not produce any new definitions of faith. Sixteen

major documents were published and those which have so far
proved to be the most influential are:

- Dogmatic Constitition on the Church (*Lumen gentium*) 1964
- Pastoral Constitution on the Church in the Modern World
  (*Gaudium et spes*) 1965
- Decree on Ecumenism 1964
- Constitution on the Sacred Liturgy 1963
- Dogmatic Constitution on Divine Revelation 1965
- Declaration on Religious Liberty 1965
- Declaration on the Relationship of the Church to Non-Christian
  Religions (*Nostra Aetate*) 1965

The authority of the Council is disclosed in the way it has been either
received or challenged. Since 1965 official documents, papal letters
and speeches, textbooks and articles make frequent reference to the
documents and use them to support whatever is being discussed.
The main challenge has come from Archbishop Marcel Lefèbvre
(d.1991). He refused to put his name to documents such as *Gaudium
et Spes* and was totally opposed to any form of ecumenical dialogue.
In 1976 he went so far as to claim that it was the Church under Pope
Paul VI that was in schism, not his own group, and acted on this
opinion later, in 1988, by consecrating four bishops. For this he
incurred excommunication, having refused many attempts to be
reconciled. In writing formally about this Pope John Paul II indicates
the authority of the Council as he sees it. In the ongoing and living
tradition 'there is a growth of insight into the realities and words that
are passed on.' He calls for 'loyalty to that tradition of the Church
authentically interpreted by the ordinary and extraordinary
magisterium of the Church, especially in the ecumenical councils
from Nicaea to Vatican II.' He asks 'theologians and experts in
ecclesiastical studies to realise that they have a contribution to make.
The breadth and depth of the teaching of the Second Vatican Council
call for a renewed effort to deepen general awareness of how the
Council is in line with tradition especially on those points of doctrine
which perhaps, because of their freshness have not been well
understood by some sections of the Church.' (Apostolic Letter *Motu
Proprio*, 2 July 1988.) We can see in these words the affirmation that
the Council went back to the origins of Catholic tradition and that
what may have seemed innovation to some was, in fact, not so.

The impact of the Council

Evaluations of the consequences of the Council for the Church differ
according to the distance from events as well as the temperament of
the critic. The Council sessions took place during what have been

called 'the turbulent sixties.' The applications of renewal were in the context of disturbances on campuses in the USA and Britain, industrial unrest particularly in France and Germany and the tensions of the Cold War. It seemed as though many of the accepted restraints in society were being overthrown. The seeds of the Council were planted in soil where plants tended to grow wild. Many Catholics were horrified by liturgical experiments, new attitudes in the religious orders, priests conspiring against bishops and what seemed to be 'the runaway Church.'

Cardinal Montini of Milan succeeded Pope John, taking the name of Pope Paul VI. He was fully in sympathy with the hopes and intentions of his predecessor but was caught up in the difficulties of making true renewal possible within the apparent chaos of a limited and distorted understanding of what this meant. By temperament he was not suited to the task because he was a worrier, and indecisive. (Pope John called him Amletico – like Hamlet, to be or not to be?) Even so, he initiated the most effective means for letting the truth of the Council be known – the translation and publication of the foundation documents. He also encouraged the study essential for their meaning to be absorbed and then applied.

In addition to the Council's documents, well over one hundred further papers have been produced setting out particular items in greater detail. This material is readily available to anybody, at least in the western world. Elsewhere the obstacles are mainly of finance and literacy and the constraints of the political situation. Pope John Paul II, while still in Poland, travelled regularly to Rome to help in preparing the documents and publicised them in his own country in a book called 'The Foundations of Renewal.'

It is inevitable that some have been disappointed that things have not moved faster and that the initial optimism and pressure for change have faded. But in such matters, and taking account of the widely different contexts of the Catholic Church throughout the world there has to be a period of stabilisation and consolidation. In certain aspects there have been lasting gains.

In 1985 the Synod of Bishops reviewed the situation. Many referred to Vatican II as 'a new Pentecost . . . which created in the Church a greater attitude of listening and of service.' The Council was seen as a light for the journey into the future. Its capacity to be like this was expressed by Cardinal O'Fiaich:

'Our aim must be to make this Synod a treasury of the living riches of Vatican II, not a tomb in which they are buried. The Synod's central message must therefore be to proclaim its adherence to the doctrine of Vatican II . . . My hope for the Synod is that it will not be a policeman signalling 'Stop' but a helpful traffic-warden supplying the Catholic Church with a road map, that is, the documents of Vatican II.'

The significance of this view is that it rests with the bishops to take the initiative in educating their clergy and laity. Their positive views of Vatican II will go far to ensuring the continuing renewal of the Church.

In 1987 the Synod's theme was *The Vocation and Mission of the Laity in the World* and it was followed by a substantial papal statement on the subject, referring extensively to Council documents. This is a formal indication of the significant part now being played by the laity at all levels. The Church is no longer described by the image of a pyramid with the laity as the base and the priests and bishops forming the peak, topped by the pope. Through baptism all share a fundamental equality as the People of God. This is the primary concept of 'Church.' The division of service as clergy or laity is a secondary matter.

The reform of the liturgy had begun before the Council, for example in increased participation by the congregation. The use of the vernacular became an obvious next step and was especially necessary for the churches in Asia and Africa. The study of scripture has been revived, for it was the Reformation which led to its taking a smaller role than in the first centuries of the Christian Church. This restoration of its rightful place has helped to improve relations between Catholics and Protestants. The use of the chalice for the laity was permitted by the Council though until 1985 it has not been the common practice.

These modifications had an immediate effect upon the laity and some found it hard to adapt. Where there was adequate explanation of the reasons for change the teaching power of the liturgy was recognised.

For non-Catholics one of the most noticeable and far-reaching consequences of the Council has been its effect on ecumenism. Pope John's experience in Bulgaria and Turkey had brought him into contact with the Orthodox Church and he realised that the wall of division could not be broken down overnight. He said, 'I try to pull out a brick here and there.' Before the Council met he set up a

Secretariat for Unity (1960) under Cardinal Bea and this at once became important because it began to explore the problems of the divided church from the standpoint of scripture and the early Church Fathers, rather than from later theological positions.

From Cardinal Bea came the most promising argument of all for inter-church dialogue. 'Non-Catholics must not be put on the same plane as the non-baptised; for they always bear, not only the name of Christ on their foreheads, but his actual image in their soul, deeply and indelibly imprinted there by baptism.' (Bea, 1963, p32) Cardinal Bea was also successful in persuading members of the Orthodox Churches to attend the Council and in obtaining places for observers from other major Christian denominations.

It was reported in 1986 that the Secretariat for Christian Unity was currently engaged in international theological dialogue with nine Christian groups (Orthodox, Orientals, Anglicans, Lutherans, Methodists, Reformed, Disciples of Christ, Baptists, Pentecostals). There have been two major agreed reports from the Anglican-Roman Catholic International Commission (ARCIC) on *Eucharist, Ministry, and Authority* (1981) and *Salvation and the Church* (1987). The Roman Catholic Church now has full membership of the Council of Churches for Britain and Ireland (which replaced the former British Council of Churches in 1991).

The pace of ecumenical progress is too slow for some, but in 1986 Pope John Paul II reaffirmed the Church's irrevocable commitment to it. The way forward will be discovered as the Church's inner renewal begins to show its influence in liturgical and biblical movements and in commitment to the Church's social teaching and activity.

Ecumenism, in the wider sense of relations with non-Christian religions, was discussed by the Council, initially in response to Jewish representations, but the scope was widened to include all major world faiths. The Council's Declaration *Nostra Aetate* states that inter-faith dialogue can advance on the basis that all that is true in other faiths is to be accepted and all past quarrels are to be set aside. It is specifically stated that responsibility for the crucifixion cannot be attributed to all the Jews at that time nor to Jews today. The Good Friday prayers have been amended in line with this: 'Let us pray for the Jewish people, the first to hear the word of God, that they may continue to grow in the love of his name and in faithfulness to his covenant.' In Britain inter-faith dialogue continues, not only with Jews but also with Muslims, and Catholics are encouraged to appreciate the spiritual enrichment which can come from knowledge of other faiths.

Significance of the Council

Whereas earlier ecumenical councils of the Church were summoned to settle major disputes, Vatican II seems to have inaugurated an extended period of argument and debate. This can be read as a sure sign of its living reality and as confirmation that internal criticisms can be made without accusations of disloyalty. The Council has been called 'the most important ecclesiastical event of this century, not just for Catholics but for all Christians' (Hastings, 1986, p525). Catholics are still working through the implications of the Council documents and Protestants have now been drawn into a reconsideration of their attitude to the Catholic Church. As a consequence they have in many cases begun to renew their own churches in a way which seems to work in the direction of reconciliation.

MANUSCRIPTS OF THE NEW TESTAMENT

While most of the authors were of Jewish origin, the New Testament itself is written in Greek, the common tongue of the Roman Empire. Over 5,000 handwritten texts survive, the large majority dating from the eighth century or later. Since the New Testament is the starting point for Christian teaching, textual critics have laboured to establish a text which is as close as possible to the wording of the original New Testament documents. Manuscripts of significant agreement have been grouped into text-types, of which three principal texts have been isolated: the Neutral (or, Alexandrian) text; the Western text; and the Byzantine (or, Lucianic) text. Canon B.H. Streeter (*The Four Gospels*, 1924) identified and described a fourth group which he deduced was the text in use at Caesarea in the third century, hence its name the Caesarean text. The most important manuscripts include:

Codex Sinaiticus, 4th century, probably written in Egypt. Contains the whole of the Greek text of the New Testament. It was discovered in 1859 in the monastery of St. Catherine at the foot of Mount Sinai. The manuscript was sold in 1933 to the Trustees of the British Museum.

Codex Vaticanus, 4th century, probably written in Alexandria. Contains the Greek text of the New Testament up to Hebrews 9.14, the remaining leaves are missing. The manuscript is now in the Vatican Library.

The readings of *Sinaiticus* and *Vaticanus* are the chief witness to the *Neutral Text*; so called (by Dr. F.J.A. Hort) because this text was believed to be less subject to editorial revision than any other.

Codex Bezae, 5th century. Contains most of the Gospels (in the order Mt., Jn., Lk., Mk.) and Acts in Greek and Latin on facing pages. Its bilingual character suggests that it was written in an area where both Greek and Latin were in use, i.e. in the West (scholars have suggested Sicily, Lyons, N. Africa and Sardinia).

Codex Bezae was presented in 1581 to Cambridge University by Theodore Beza who had discovered it in Lyons in 1562. The manuscript is the chief witness to the Western Text.

Codex Alexandrinus, 5th century, probably written in Egypt. Contains most of the Greek text of the New Testament and perhaps the best text of Revelation. In the Gospels the Codex follows the *Lucianic Text*, i.e. the text of the Greek Bible as revised by Lucian of Antioch (d.312). Lucian's text is represented by the large majority of surviving Greek manuscripts. *Codex Alexandrinus* is housed in the British Museum.

Less complete New Testament manuscripts date back even earlier. One fragment of the Gospel of John, now in the John Rylands Library, Manchester, has been assigned to the first half of the second century. It is the earliest known manuscript of any part of the New Testament. The Chester Beatty papyri (after A. Chester Beatty who acquired them in 1931) contain portions of the Gospels, Acts, the Pauline epistles and Revelation, all dating from the first half of the third century. The Bodmer papyri (after Martin Bodmer who acquired them for his library in Geneva) include a manuscript of the Fourth Gospel of about A.D.200 which survives nearly complete, and another written in the third century which contains part of Luke and John. Because they are a century or more older than the earliest vellum manuscripts, these papyrus codices are valuable evidence for the text of the New Testament.

GLOSSARY

apocalyptic (Gk. *apokalypsis*, a 'revelation' or 'unveiling').
Apocalyptic literature claims to reveal things which are normally hidden and to unveil the future. Daniel and Revelation are examples in the Bible.

apostasy the deliberate abandonment of belief made by a former believer.

dualism the view that there are two opposite and independently existing principles that go to form everything, e.g. good and evil, spirit and matter.

eschatology (Gk. *eschatos*, 'last', and *logos*, 'discourse'): teaching/ideas about the end period of history or existence.

heterodox holding opinions contrary to accepted belief.

kerygma ('proclamation'). In the New Testament the *kerygma* is the good news of God's activity in the life, death and resurrection of Jesus.

logia ('sayings'). In New Testament criticism the term is applied to the sayings of Jesus which circulated in the early Church.

proselyte a convert to any faith or sect. In biblical studies the term refers especially to Gentiles who became Jews.

BIBLIOGRAPHY

HISTORICAL, CULTURAL AND RELIGIOUS BACKGROUND

C.K. Barrett, *The New Testament Background: Selected Documents*,
S.P.C.K., 1957.
E. Lohse, *The New Testament Environment*, S.C.M., 1980.
B. Reicke, *The New Testament Era*, A. and C. Black, 1969.

INTRODUCTION

R.F. Collins, *Introduction to the New Testament*, S.C.M., 1983.
W.G. Kümmel, *Introduction to the New Testament*, S.C.M., 1966.

THE DIVERSITY OF THE NEW TESTAMENT: CRITICAL METHODS.

R. Davidson and A. Leaney, *Biblical Criticism*, Pelican, 1970.
M. Dibelius, *From Tradition to Gospel*, Nicholson and Watson, 1934.
J.H. Hayes and C.R. Holladay, *Biblical Exegesis: A Beginner's
Handbook*, S.C.M., 1983.
I.H. Marshall (ed.), *New Testament Interpretation*, Paternoster, 1977.
N. Perrin, *What is Redaction Criticism?*, S.P.C.K., 1970.

THE UNITY OF THE NEW TESTAMENT: THEOLOGY

R. Bultmann, *Theology of the New Testament*, 2 vols., S.C.M., 1952.
H. Conzelmann, *An Outline of the Theology of the New Testament*,
S.C.M., 1968.
J.D.G. Dunn, *Unity and Diversity in the New Testament*, S.C.M., 1977.
J. Jeremias, *New Testament Theology*, vol.1, S.C.M., 1972.
W.G. Kümmel, *Theology of the New Testament*, S.C.M., 1974.

THE PERSON AND MINISTRY OF JESUS

G. Aulén, *Jesus in contemporary historical research*, S.P.C.K., 1976.
C.H. Dodd, *The Founder of Christianity*, Collins, 1971.
C.H. Dodd, *The Parables of the Kingdom*, Nisbet, 1955.
R.H. Fuller, *The Foundations of the New Testament Christology*, Fontana,
1965.
J. Jeremias, *The Parables of Jesus*, S.C.M., 1972.

E. Linneman, *Jesus of the Parables: Introduction and Exposition*, S.P.C.K., 1966.

N. Perrin, *Rediscovering the Teaching of Jesus*, S.C.M., 1967.

G. Vermes, *Jesus the Jew: A Historian's Reading of the Gospels*, Collins, 1973.

EARLIEST CHRISTIANITY

R.E. Brown, *The Churches the Apostles Left Behind*, Chapman, 1984.

S. Brown, *The Origins of Christianity*, Oxford, 1984.

F.F. Bruce, *Men and Movements in the Primitive Church*, Paternoster, 1979.

G.B. Caird, *The Apostolic Age*, Duckworth, 1955.

J.D.G. Dunn, *The Partings of the Ways*, S.C.M., 1992.

E. Pagels, *The Gnostic Gospels*, Weidenfeld and Nicolson, 1979.

K. Rudolph, *Gnosis*, T and T. Clark, 1983.

R. McL. Wilson, *Gnosis and the New Testament*, Blackwell, 1968.

CONSTANTINE AND CHRISTIANITY

T.D. Barnes, *Constantine and Eusebius*, Harvard, 1981.

H. Chadwick, *The Early Church*, Penguin, 1967.

H. Dorries, *Constantine the Great*, Harper and Row, 1972.

W.H.C. Frend, *The rise of Christianity*, Darton, Longman and Todd, 1984.

J.N.D. Kelly, *Early Christian Creeds*, Longman, 1972.

R. MacMullen, *Constantine*, Weidenfeld and Nicolson, 1970.

J. Stevenson (ed.), *A new Eusebius*, S.P.C.K., 1957.

THE GREAT SCHISM

J.F. Bethune-Baker, *Introduction to the Early History of Christian Doctrine*, Methuen, 1951.

G. Every, *Misunderstandings between East and West*, Lutterworth, 1965.

K.S. Latourette, *A history of Christianity*, Eyre and Spottiswoode, 1954.

J. Meyendorff, *Byzantine Theology*, New York, Fordham University Press, 1974.

A. Schmemann, *The historical road of eastern orthodoxy*, London, Harvill Press, 1963.

R.W. Southern, *Western Society and the Church in the Middle Ages*, Penguin, 1970.

THE REFORMATION

H. Bettenson (ed.), *Documents of the Christian Church*, O.U.P., 1943.

O. Chadwick, *The Reformation*, Penguin, 1964.

A.G. Dickens, *Martin Luther*, London, English University Press, 1967.

H.J. Hillerbrand, *The world of the Reformation*, Dent, 1975.

E. Iserloh, J. Glazik, H. Jedin, *Reformation and Counter-Reformation*, Burns and Oates, 1980.

A. McGrath, *Reformation Thought*, Blackwell, 1988.

H.A. Oberman, *The dawn of the Reformation*, T. and T. Clark, 1986.

J.M. Todd, *Reformation*, Darton, Longman and Todd, 1972.

MEETING TWENTIETH CENTURY CHALLENGES

A. Bea, *The unity of Christians*, Chapman, 1963.

T. Best (ed.), *Vancouver to Canberra, 1983-1990*, W.C.C. Publications, 1990.

C. Butler, *The theology of Vatican II*, Darton, Longman and Todd, 1967.

A. Flannery (ed.), *Vatican Council II, The Conciliar and Post Conciliar Documents*, New York, Costello Pub. Co., 1984.

A. Hastings, *A history of English Christianity (1920-1985)*, Collins, 1986.

P. Hebblethwaite, *John XXIII Pope of the Council*, Chapman, 1964.

H.G.G. Herklots, *Looking at Evanston*, S.C.M., 1954.

D.E. Johnson (ed.), *Uppsala to Nairobi, 1968-1975*, S.P.C.K., 1975.

Lima text: *Baptism, Eucharist and Ministry*, W.C.C. Publications, 1990.

New Delhi Speaks, S.C.M., 1962.

V. Nichols (ed.), *Reflections: how 26 churches see their life and mission*, Inter-Church Process, 1986.

D.M. Paton (ed.), *Breaking Barriers, Nairobi 1975*, S.P.C.K., 1976.

R. Rouse and S.C. Neill, *A History of the Ecumenical Movement (1517-1948)*, S.P.C.K., 1967.

A.J. Van der Bent, *The Utopia of World Community*, S.C.M., 1973.

M. Van Elderen, *Introducing the W.C.C.*, W.C. Publications, 1990.

A.R. Vidler, *The Church in an Age of Revolution*, Penguin, 1961.

INDEX